ENDORSEMENTS

I came to know Pastor George Proctor when he submitted a response to one of the religious columns he had read in the Fort Scott Tribune. I spoke with him and he asked if he could write a column, too, maybe once a month. I welcomed his idea and looked forward to offering readers a new perspective. I received a column the next week, and the next week, and the next. So it hasn't been a monthly column, but a column that is shared as often as Pastor Proctor is able. I have often smiled as I know God is guiding Pastor Proctor to share with readers His Word and we need that Word often.

These are trying times, and Pastor Proctor reminds us of God's promise of grace, which will carry us through those trying times. We need reminders that we need not worry about what a new year will bring or that we need to burden ourselves with worries of any kind. That message has always given me comfort.

Pastor Proctor's Nuggets to Live By are practical messages for everyone. You go to church every week, tithe, maybe even sing in the choir. You're a pretty good Christian, right? Pastor Proctor has often reminded me that we are all sinners, and none of us is a perfect Christian. But God is there for us and so is Pastor Proctor, sharing a "nugget" to remind us how to live as better Christians.

We all need a nugget or two or three. I hope you, too, will find Pastor Proctor's words a blessing in your life.

—**Tammy Helm**,
Managing Editor
Fort Scott Tribune

This book is dedicated to my lovely wife, Willetta—an awesome blessing from God that has been my love and confidant.

Special thanks to my parents, George and Corine, whom I miss dearly, for they were truly a blessing to me! Also, my sons George III, Nicholas, Nathaniel, Darrell and daughter, Shauna, of whom I am very proud and proud to be their dad!

I want to also dedicate this book to the Saints of God that have a sincere desire to draw closer to God through an insatiable urge to study and embrace His Word!

As well as to those who are yet lost and "tired of being tired." Ready to seek divine answers that the world is not equipped to provide. Answers that have been waiting for you since before the beginning of time and are relevant for today and eternity!

Rev. George Proctor
Pastor,
United Missionary Baptist Church
& Olathe Family Worship Center
Moderator, Neosho Vally District

Nuggets
to Live By

Nuggets to Live By

PASTOR GEORGE PROCTOR

EQUIP PRESS

Colorado Springs

Nuggets to live by

Copyright © 2018, Pastor George Proctor

All rights reserved. No part of this publication may be reproduced, distributed, or transmitted in any form or by any means, without prior written permission.

Published by Equip Press, Colorado Springs, CO

Scripture quotations marked (ESV) are taken from The ESV® Bible (The Holy Bible, English Standard Version®) copyright © 2001 by Crossway, a publishing minis-try of Good News Publishers. ESV® Text Edition: 2011. The ESV® text has been reproduced in cooperation with and by permission of Good News Publishers.
Unauthorized reproduction of this publication is prohibited. Used by permission.
All rights reserved.

Scripture quotations marked (KJV) are taken from the King James Bible. Accessed on Bible Gateway at www.BibleGateway.com.

Scripture quotations marked (NASB) are taken from the New American Standard Bible® (NASB), copyright © 1960, 1962, 1963, 1968, 1971, 1972, 1973, 1975, 1977, 1995 by The Lockman Foundation, www.Lockman.org. Used by permission.

Scripture quotations marked (NIV) are taken from the Holy Bible, New International Version. Copyright © 1973, 1978, 1984, 2011 by Biblica, Inc.® Used by permission.
All rights reserved worldwide.

Scripture quotations marked (NKJV) are taken from the New King James Version®.
Copyright © 1982 by Thomas Nelson, Inc. Used by permission. All rights reserved.

Scripture quotations marked (NLT) are taken from the Holy Bible, New Living Translation, copyright © 1996, 2004, 2015 by Tyndale House Foundation. Used by permission of Tyndale House Publishers, Inc., Carol Stream, Illinois 60188. All rights reserved.

Scripture quotations marked (NRSV) are taken from the New Revised Standard Version Bible, copyright © 1989 the Division of Christian Education of the National Council of the Churches of Christ in the United States of America. Used by permission. All rights reserved.

First Edition: 2018
Nuggets to Live By / Pastor George Proctor
Paperback ISBN: 978-1-946453-43-3
eBook ISBN: 978-1-946453-44-0

EQUIP PRESS
Colorado Springs

fOREWORD

Many prospectors traveled West during the California Gold Rush in 1848. Their hope was to find gold, become rich, and have a better life for their families. One of the easiest methods was gold panning where large clumps of soil and gravel were put into a pan. Water was used to shake and sift the dirt and mud away with the anticipation that the fleck of a shiny gold nugget would appear. The work was often backbreaking and few were successful. Some never found what they were hoping for.

I see my wonderful husband, the Rev. George Proctor, as a modern-day gold miner. He spends countless hours studying and sifting through the Bible to find little pieces of golden nuggets that will illuminate God's Word to anyone who has a desire and an open heart to receive it.

He doesn't keep these nuggets to himself for his own personal enjoyment and enrichment. He shares them freely so that others may also become rich in the knowledge of the Lord. The recipients of these nuggets see God's Word in a whole different light and have an insatiable urge to learn more, so they may have a closer relationship with God. They will come to know that the riches here on Earth are only temporary and can't nearly compare to the riches God has laid up for us in heaven.

My prayer is that when you read these *Nuggets to Live By*, you will become strengthened and the Holy Bible will suddenly become less challenging and more inviting to you. You will begin to look with new eyes with confidence at the significance and importance of simple little words. Stories and passages across all the Bible's sixty-six books will suddenly start to "connect" and make sense. After reading these "nuggets," you will find yourself digging and searching the Bible for your own personal nuggets of gold. You will be astounded how something you read two weeks ago can have a totally different meaning today. As you evolve, the Word of God will evolve with you for wherever you are at any given stage of your life. You will find that something you read today may be just what you needed to get you through the challenges of the day. That's why you should <u>never</u> stop reading and studying God's Word.

This book is not a substitute for the Bible, but a key to unlock some of the challenges you may have experienced as you tried to study on your own. *Nuggets to Live By* is a beautiful treasure chest of precious jewels to enrich your life and hopefully the lives of those you know and love. You don't have to travel far to get these riches. They are all right here for you just for the taking!

— *Mrs. Willetta Proctor*

CONTENTS

	Foreword	9
1.	**Messages To The Saints Of God**	**15**
	Why Call Me Saint?	17
	Saints, Do You Fear Satan or Does Satan Fear You?	21
	Where Is the Evidence of Your Faith, Saints?	25
	What Is Man That Thou Art Mindful of Him?	29
	Are You Focused on What the World Is Coming To . . . ?	33
	Are You on Satan's "Hit List"?	37
	Has Your Ship Come In?	41
	Drinking from the Cup of Salvation	45
	Draw Me Nearer, Precious Lord!	49
	Depressed, Are You?	53
	Being Prepared for Satan's Attacks	57
	Are You Making a Deal with the Devil?	61
	A Transformed Woman	65
	A Matter of the Heart	69
	Are You the Apple of Our God's Eye?	73
	Are You "Such a Man"?	77
	A Love Letter in Troubled Times	81

	A Bright and Shining Star for My Lord	85
	. . . Because He First Loved Me (Part 1)	89
	. . . Because He First Loved Me (Part 2)	93
	Avoiding a Life of Chaos	97
	Be Inspired as You Wait and Trust	101
	Becoming a Friend of God	105
	Daily Our God Saves Us from Ourselves	109
	Caring for the Eye of God	113
	Earth's Universal Song	117
	Faith Honors God and God Honors Faith	121
	Glory Be to the Name of the Lord!	125
	God Does Not Comfort Us to Be Comfortable	129
2.	**God Is!**	**133**
	God Is!	135
	God's Promises Can Buckle Your Knees	139
	God Only Is Our Present Help and Our Eternal Hope	143
	God, Our Wonderful Deliverer!	147
	God Says, "Hold My Hand and Walk with Me"	151
	God Yearns for a Relationship with His Children	155
	How Well Do You Really Know God?	159
	God's Deep and Rich Wisdom	163
	God's Deep and Rich Knowledge	167
	Great Is Thy Faithfulness	171
	He Is Slow but Never Late	175
	It's Raining Blessings for God's People!	181
	No Better Hands to Put Your Life in Than Jesus'	185
	One on One with Our Father	189
	Our God Forgives . . . Do You? (Part 1)	193
	Our God Forgives . . . Do You? (Part 1)	197

CONTENTS

	Our God Forgives . . . Do You? (Part 3)	201
	Our God Is a Consuming Fire	207
	Our God Is Not a Man	213
	Our God Sings and Abundantly Much More	217
	Our Holy God	221
	Our Thirst Quencher	225
	Perfect in All His Ways (Part 1)	229
	Perfect in All His Ways (Part 2)	235
	Perfect Peace	241
3.	**Sainthood**	**245**
	Saints, Is God Real in Your Life Today?	247
	Saints, There Is More to Life	251
	The Power Within (Continued)	255
	Rejoice in the Lord, Saints!	259
	Resting in Green Pastures of Expectation	263
	Saints, Are You Still on the Run?	267
	Saints, We Are Somebody!	271
	Saints, You Are Not Alone	275
	Saints, Becoming More like Jesus in Our Praise	279
	Saints, Do You Have More Faith in Man Than in God?	283
	Saints, Do You Really Know the Power, Will, and Love of God?	287
	Saints, Rely on the Strong for Strength	291
	Saints, Stir the Kool-Aid!	295
	Saints, We Have Our Marching Orders	299
	Saints, We Have the Best Benefits Package	305
	Saints, Who Knows and Loves You Best?	309
	Satan Can Hurt a Well-Dressed Soldier	313
	Satan, You Better Help the Bear!	317

	Snatching Victory from the Jaws of Defeat	321
	Staying in the Center of the Road	327
	Taking God's Kindness for Weakness	331
	The Image of a Christian	335
	Wait on the Lord, Saints!	339
	Why Do You Go to Church, Saints?	343
4.	**Prayer and Patience**	**347**
	It's Prayer Time, Saints!	349
	The Prayer of One	353
	Praying without Faith Is Really Begging	357
	Praying without Patience Is for Wimps	361
	The Promise of Answered Prayer	365
	The Promise of Grace to Endure	369
	The Secret Prayer of a Father	373
	The Perfect Work of Patience for the Apostle Paul	377
	The Perfect Work of Patience for God's First Evangelist	381
	The Perfect Work of Patience for Job (Part 1)	385
	The Perfect Work of Patience for Job (Part 2)	389
	The Perfect Work of Patience for the Saints	393

1

MESSAGES TO THE SAINTS OF GOD

NUGGETS TO LIVE BY

WHY CALL ME SAINT?

Saints, some have asked me this very question. Well let us look at the reason many of you are in fact Saints:

NUGGET ONE

The Greek word *hagios* and the Hebrew word *kadosh* both in their various forms mean holiness, Saints, and sanctification—which basically means those who are called such are set apart, separated, and different.

Those who have accepted Jesus Christ as their Savior and Lord have been called out of this world, separated, and made new. Old things have passed away, and all things become new by the Spirit which now dwells within us.

2 Corinthians 5:17-18 (KJV)
[17] Therefore if any man be in Christ, he is a new creature: old things are passed away; behold, all things are become new. [18] And all things are of God, who hath reconciled us to himself by Jesus Christ, and hath given to us the ministry of reconciliation . . .

Note, Saints, that God has positioned those who have accepted His plan of salvation through His Son Jesus Christ as new! Now as new creatures set apart by God, we have become Saints! Saints called out by God for His purpose! Hence, while we are in this world we are no longer of this world but separated to do the will of God.

We as believers have become a new holy nation of Saints, a peculiar people. We are no longer black, white, Jew or Greek, but Saints in one army with *"one Lord, one faith, one baptism, one God and Father of all, who is above all, and through all, and in you all"* (Eph. 4:5–6).

Saints, that is our "position" as believers, but we are to become much more than that as we grow in the knowledge of God and our calling as Saints of God. This is the very reason I am sharing these "nuggets" and writing this book, *Nuggets to Live By* . . .

NUGGET TWO

Now that you understand that we are positioned as Saints of God, we must realize our responsibility as Saints. As Saints we are to allow the Spirit that has been placed within us to set us apart for God every day, minute by minute! As Saints we should with zeal and purpose seek the Holy Spirit in us to change us as we long to live spiritual lives for our Lord, no longer fleshly lives for the world that God has called us out of to serve only Him.

Ephesians 2:10–13 (KJV)

*[10] For we are his workmanship, created in Christ Jesus unto good works, which God hath before ordained that we should walk in them. [11] Wherefore remember, that ye being in time past Gentiles in the flesh, who are called **Uncircumcision** by that which is called the **Circumcision***

in the flesh made by hands; [12] *That at that time ye were without Christ, being aliens from the commonwealth of Israel, and strangers from the covenants of promise, having no hope, and without God in the world:* [13] *But now in Christ Jesus ye who sometimes were far off are made nigh by the blood of Christ.*

Therefore, when I call you Saints as believers of God through the blood of Jesus Christ, I am recognizing that God has positioned you as such, SAINT! However, that is only the beginning because you now must take an account as to where you are in your Sainthood.

Have you allowed the Holy Spirit that God has placed in you to change you day by day for His glory, or are you stagnant in your growth in the knowledge of God? Have you allowed and recognized the Holy Spirit in your life guiding you through your day-to-day trials to bring you into a more personal intimate relationship with God?

If your answer is yes then the Scripture is clear—as Saints we have responsibility:

Psalm 116:12–14 (KJV)
[12] *What shall I render unto the LORD for all his benefits toward me?*
[13] *I will take the cup of salvation, and call upon the name of the LORD.*
[14] *I will pay my vows unto the LORD now in the presence of all his people.*

God Bless

NUGGETS TO LIVE BY

SAINTS, DO YOU FEAR SATAN OR DOES SATAN FEAR YOU?

Saints, I pray you all know that God has not given us the spirit of fear! Instead He has given us one way to surely cause Satan to tremble in fear of us!

The best way to strike utter fear in Satan is to win souls for Christ! In Acts 1:8 Jesus' last words on Earth before His ascension, told us this very thing:

Acts 1:8 (KJV)
8 "But ye shall receive power, after that the Holy Ghost is come upon you: and ye shall be witnesses unto me both in Jerusalem, and in all Judaea, and in Samaria, and unto the uttermost part of the earth."

NUGGET ONE

Saints, Jesus gave us an equipping Spirit, not a spirit of fear! This Spirit is to equip you to cause Satan himself to shake in fear as you win souls for Christ. Yet many have this power lying dormant within them because they never tell the story of salvation to the lost. Is that you, Saint?

🏷 NUGGET TWO

Notice in the text that Jesus' last word was that we be witnesses unto Him. Saints, that word *witness* is a Greek word used for *martyr*. Meaning that Jesus is telling us that we are to be prepared to sacrifice in spreading the good news of Jesus Christ!

Yes, Saints, we are to sacrifice for the cause of Christ who poured out Himself for us! Paul puts it this way when responding to those who begged and cried that he not go into the pending danger waiting for him in Jerusalem (Acts 21). Paul assured them that he was prepared to be put in chains and even to die for the cause of Christ!

Saints, are you prepared to get out of your chairs, turn off the TV, leave the golf course, or get out of your pew and tell this dark needful world about Jesus? How many of you go to church week after week and never invite an unbeliever to come and hear the Word of God?

Some of you may say, "Pastor, I cannot quote Scriptures like you can or quote Roman's Road . . ."

🏷 NUGGET THREE

Saints, look at the text! Jesus says that we are to be witnesses unto Him. There is nothing there saying you should be quoting Scripture or Roman's Road. While knowing those would come in time as you trust in the Holy Spirit who dwells within you, praise God! But until then Jesus is telling us before He ascended that we should tell the world what He did for YOU!

Saints, nobody can tell your heartfelt story of your deliverance better than you! Have you shared it with a lost soul recently? Have you shared it at all this year? How many souls have you brought to Jesus by you own testimony? Is there evidence of that in your church? Or are you yet an "undercover Christian"?

John the Baptist in Matthew 3:11 says that he baptized with water unto repentance but He that cometh after him is mightier than him, and He will baptize with the Holy Ghost and with fire! Saints, are you using that "FIRE" that dwells within you to cause Satan to tremble in fear? If so, praise God! If not, why not? For you are without excuse, Saint!

I leave you with this Scripture and pray that it pricks your hearts, Saints, for this *world is getting darker by the minute!* Not because Satan is doing such a good job *BUT BECAUSE SAINTS ARE NOT SPREADING WITH THE FIRE OF THE HOLY SPIRIT THAT DWELLS WITHIN THEM! FOR GREATER IS HE THAT IS IN YOU THAN HE THAT IS IN THE WORLD! GET UP, UNDERCOVER CHRISTIANS, AND TELL THE WORLD WHAT JESUS HAS DONE FOR YOU . . .*

1 Corinthians 15:58 (KJV)
[58] "Therefore, my beloved brethren, be ye steadfast, unmovable, always abounding in the work of the Lord, forasmuch as ye know that your labour is not in vain in the Lord."

God Bless!

NUGGETS TO LIVE BY

WHERE IS THE EVIDENCE OF FAITH, SAINTS?

Saints, if God was to ask you to demonstrate the evidence of your faith, how would you begin? Would you say that you pray daily? That you live right? That you love your neighbor? That you feed the poor?

Another question, have you ever found yourself in such a predicament that only your faith could carry you through? Well, Saints, in John chapter 4 there was such a situation experienced by an official whose son was dying.

This man had only heard about Jesus and yet demonstrated remarkable faith that not only saved him but his entire household!

NUGGET ONE

This official at some point turned his ear to the Word of Jesus! At some point he had heard about Jesus and His healing and deliverance. In a moment of weakness and need, the official turned to Jesus in faith.

Imagine, the official left his dying son to go to Jesus for help! Stepping out on faith and not his position. Saints, this is the first evidence of our faith—the decision to step out on faith turning all our cares upon Him, seeking Him and His guidance, deliverance, and healing.

This official left his dying son and journeyed almost a day's journey. Imagine what could be going on inside his heart. Has he left his son alive for the last time? What if Jesus said no? What if he could not find Jesus in time?

Saints, faith is what sought Jesus! Has your faith sought Jesus in your times of struggle?

NUGGET TWO

Saints, the official demonstrated his faith by his belief and persistence. Jesus said to the official that he needed "signs and wonders" and would not believe. In other words, Jesus did not want to convince the official by "signs and wonders" but Jesus wanted the man to reveal his total faith in Jesus. Many would have left Jesus at that point. Imagine traveling all day to hear Jesus say this!

Saints, how many times do you give up on your prayers because there is no answer received as timely as you expect it? Or pray that God give you a sign when He has already given you a promise?

The text says that the official was persistent, recognizing that Jesus was the only one who could save His son, and he believed that His very presence was the answer! That's belief and persistent faith!

That was the evidence Jesus was looking for, Saints! Saints, when you pray, do you thank God in advance for His answer? Thanking Him because you already trust that whatever the answer, it is on the way, and it is the most perfect answer because it is the will of God for you!

NUGGET THREE

Even though the official wanted Jesus to come with him, he knew that Jesus' answer was the best answer. Instead of accompanying him, Jesus told the official to "Go," his son had been healed! Oh Saints, the official revealed an obedient trusting faith. Imagine his walk home! He was obedient in trusting the Word of Jesus, trusting the faithfulness of Jesus. Not "signs and wonders" but the Word of Jesus!

Saints, how many times when you pray do you remain in doubt of the faithfulness of our God? Not trusting His promise that He will never leave you nor forsake you? That He will not suffer you to be tempted beyond what you can bear? And that He will make a way of escape for you? Saints, that is because of His love just for you!

Saints, what is the evidence of **YOUR** faith? Is it a wavering faith? Is it a faith seeking "signs and wonders"? Or is it a faith trusting in the faithfulness of God? A faith so demonstrated that it can win souls for Christ!

John 4:53 (KJV)
53 "So the father knew that it was at the same hour, in which Jesus said unto him, Thy son liveth: and himself believed, and his whole house."

Saints, let the evidence of your faith win souls for the kingdom!

God Bless!

NUGGETS TO LIVE BY

WHAT IS MAN THAT THOU ART MINDFUL OF HIM?

Saints, on a few occasions I have been blessed with the opportunity to spend time in the country. On those occasions I have experienced what I refer to as "David moments."

These usually come when I lie under a star-filled sky, whether at youth camp or riding with my Christian motorcyclist chapter, or on the side of the road with my sons as we headed back to their college.

I picture David lying on the ground under a clear sky, filled with stars, when he writes Psalm 8. The awesomeness of God's creation causes David to enter a "Selah moment," and yet he says that God's *"glory is above the heavens"*!

NUGGET ONE

Saints, David is pondering the fact that no matter how magnificent God's creation is, it still cannot begin to touch His glory! Saints, even the billions and billions of stars, galaxies, and planets only scrape the surface of the magnificent glory of our Almighty God!

Wow, Saints! Imagine David lying there recognizing that God Himself placed every star, galaxy, planet, moon, and sun with His fingers! Saints, our God, according to David, did not fling these into the heavens to fall where they may but took time to place them exactly where he wanted them just for you and me!

NUGGET TWO

Psalm 8:3 (KJV)
³ "When I consider thy heavens, the work of thy fingers, the moon and the stars, which thou hast ordained..."

Saints, the word *ordained* means to set in place. Our God set each in place just for you and I. Can you see David lying there in awe of the glory of God? Any wonder why David started the Psalm with, **"LORD, our Lord, how excellent is thy name in all the earth..."**?

However, when David contemplates all this he begins to be even more amazed that God has a role for man, that God has even a thought for man. That God Himself would take the time to think of man! *What and why would our Lord think of us in the midst of such an awesome creation?*

NUGGET THREE

Jeremiah 29:11 (KJV)
¹¹ "For I know the thoughts that I think toward you, saith the LORD, thoughts of peace, and not of evil, to give you an expected end."

Saints, Jeremiah asked the same question, and look at the answer our Lord gave him. Our God *knows* the thoughts He has for us! There is NO DOUBT of His love that is demonstrated by His thoughts *for PEACE* for us, His children! The book of Philippians calls it a peace that surpasses all understanding. A peace as we walk this dusty ground called earth, and a peace even as we are being chasten of the Lord! Because our Lord will never chasten His Saints as He chastens the world (1 Corinthians).

Finally, David says, who is man that thou *"visitest him"*?

Saints, who are we that God in all His magnificence and glory would take the time to visit us? Take the time in every one of our circumstances to be an ever-present God? Take the time as we walk this earth to listen and answer our prayers? Take the time to hold our hands, dry our tears, and to provide daily blessings and mercies new each morning? Who is this frail and weak man?

Friends, simply put, our Lord is LOVE! The best visit was God sending His Son, Jesus Christ! This visit changed things for all mankind. It provided a way to an eternal life with our God!

Have you accepted this visit? Have you accepted Jesus Christ? Perhaps you need to lie under the stars and read Psalm 8.

Psalm 8:9 (KJV)
[9] *"O LORD our Lord, how excellent is thy name in all the earth!"*

God Bless!

ARE YOU FOCUSED ON WHAT THE WORLD IS COMING TO . . . ?

O r, Saints, are you focused on who came to the world?
Many times, I hear Christians in the heat of worldly battles say with the deepest soul- wrenching expletive, "Oh, Jesus, *please* hurry back!" I have also done this from the very bottom of my soul many times.

Especially when I see young Christians being killed for their beliefs during this time in our history and adults pointing fingers at whether gun control is or is not the answer. Meanwhile our children are killed as we grow numb to the senseless killing. Saints, Satan is truly on his J-O-B!

But Saints, are you really ready for the return of Jesus Christ . . . really? How do you know? Why focus on what this world is coming to when it is clear scripturally where it is going. Rather, let us focus as the children of the Most High and Merciful God on who He sent to the world!

NUGGET ONE

Titus 2:11 says that the very GRACE of God appeared to all men! This unmerited favor came to all men who were doomed to hell because of the sin in man. This awesome GRACE came to the world in the person of Jesus Christ our Savior, who came to redeem man back to our Father.

God our Father offered His very best GRACE, in His most perfect son Jesus Christ—an unblemished Lamb led to be slaughtered for us!

Titus 2:11 (KJV)
[11] "For the grace of God that bringeth salvation hath appeared to all men . . ."

Praise God, Saints, the redemption did not stop there! Paul, in Titus, further reminds us that God's most awesome GRACE in the person of His Son *teaches* us!

NUGGET TWO

Saints, when you attend events such as bridal showers, picnics, sports tailgates, etc., you prepare meticulously to make sure you have everything to make it a success, amen? You make lists, pack items early in the car, and make sure the car is fueled and ready to go . . .

But what do you do to prepare for the biggest event in your eternal life? Here is the list prepared by the GRACE of God, Jesus Christ:

Titus 2:12 (KJV)
[12] "Teaching us that, denying ungodliness and worldly lusts, we should live soberly, righteously, and godly, in this present world . . ."

Saints, while in this present world we must focus on **THIS** list! When the trumpet sounds, what will you be found doing? Are you really ready for the return of Jesus Christ . . . really?

Ah, but Saints, not to worry! Jesus had to remind those hard-headed Pharisees that the Law only points out the sinfulness and wretched state of man. The Law was to point man to the fact of his vital need of a Savior! Saints, YES, we are to deny anything that is contrary to God and His commandments, and YES, we are to live our lives with temperance and righteously in this present world recognizing we need the blood of our Savior Jesus Christ to justify us before the father!

NUGGET THREE

Saints, when we really realize how vital it is for us to rely on our Savior and His teachings then YES, we are ready for His return! However, if we are focused on anything else as a distraction from this, then are we truly ready for His return?

Trusting and focusing on the most awesome GRACE that came to the world and abiding by His teachings and recognizing how much we need His blood to justify, we now can . . . well you read it!

Titus 2:13 (KJV)
13 "Looking for that blessed hope, and the glorious appearing of the great God and our Saviour Jesus Christ . . ."

God Bless!

NUGGETS TO LIVE BY

ARE YOU ON SATAN'S "HIT LIST"?

My friend, please allow me to let you in on a little secret: if you are seeking your crown and are heavenbound, you are on Satan's "Hit List." If you are not, you are on Satan's "Guest List."

Those who are on Satan's guest list are no longer targets but associates. Those who are genuine believers seeking their crown are constantly (I say CONSTANTLY, repeatedly without fail) being targeted by the Evil One!

As heavenbound Saints, we know that Satan is working overtime on his Hit List. Oh, but Saints, we have a way to tell Satan to go to hell!

📖 NUGGET ONE

There was a man who was richly blessed by God and was on Satan's Hit List. Satan even accused God of bribing this man for his faith by blessing him. God allowed Satan to try this man, and Satan went immediately into "attack mode," leaving no stone unturned.

Ah, but even though this man, Job, was receiving messenger after messenger with the bad news of his blessings being stripped from him, Job would not curse God as Satan said he would.

So how did Job tell Satan to go to hell? Look with me:

Job 1:20–21 (KJV)
²⁰ "Then Job arose, and rent his mantle, and shaved his head, and fell down upon the ground, and worshipped, ²¹ And said, 'Naked came I out of my mother's womb, and naked shall I return thither: the LORD gave, and the LORD hath taken away; blessed be the name of the LORD.'"

During Satan's attack, Job told Satan of his ultimate fate by praising God. Saints, the way we remind Satan of his ultimate fate is to praise our God!

Saints, during the State Baptist Convention in Emporia, Kansas, I spoke on the topic that "We are to get our praise on, no matter what's going on." That is exactly what Job did! In front of all the messengers, Job expressed hurt, but he never accused or cursed God. Instead, he "put his praise on, no matter what was going on!"

However, I know there remain a few skeptics lingering out there saying that no one has faced such disaster as Job.

Well, let me ask you another question, Saints. Have you ever felt as if the rich well-to-do unbelievers are being blessed more than you? Even those who profess belief but live their lives reflecting quite the opposite while you are being persecuted from every side?

🪙 NUGGET TWO

Saints, there was a heavenbound Saint by the name of Asaph who was so upset about witnessing this happening to himself and other Christians that he said he found himself envious of these wicked people. Oh, but look at what he said:

> **Psalm 73:17–20 (KJV)**
> *¹⁷ "Until I went into the sanctuary of God; then understood I their end.*
> *¹⁸ Surely thou didst set them in slippery places: thou castedst them down into destruction. ¹⁹ How are they brought into desolation, as in a moment! They are utterly consumed with terrors. ²⁰ As a dream when one awaketh; so, O Lord, when thou awakest, thou shalt despise their image."*

Saints, Asaph went into the presence of God in praise. Asaph "put his praise on no matter what was going on!"

Saints, with the ugliness of this world being put on "Front Street" for all to see, our political, judicial, and even our law enforcement systems, we must learn to praise God! Asaph and Job were richly blessed by God despite what was going on at the time.

Today, Saints, we may have a new president, an unfair legal and political system, and an unaccountable law enforcement system, but make no doubt about it, God is still in control! The same God who delivered Job and Asaph is the same God today!

Saints, we must "put our praise on, no matter what is going on!"

> **Hebrews 10:23 (KJV)**
> *²³ "Let us hold fast the profession of our faith without wavering; (for he is faithful that promised)..."*

MORE THAN EVER, SAINTS!

God Bless!

HAS YOUR SHIP COME IN?

Saints, back in the day people used to say the phrase, "I can't wait until my ship comes in." Some of you may have used this phrase yourself. This phrase usually denoted some miraculous moment that would be life changing for the one saying it.

It could be a legal settlement, a new professional position, or a lucrative contract. It always referred to something life changing that would be of great benefit.

Saints, in the Gospels of **Matthew (8:23–27), Mark (4:35–41), and Luke (8:22–25),** God had these disciples pen a miraculous event but only Mark's account mentions two key nuggets—two key nuggets for those seeking a miracle in their life. Are you seeking such a miracle? The question is, "Has your ship come in?"

In the text we see that Jesus was tired from preaching and teaching all day. He was so tired that He was taken just as he was in a ship to cross the sea to the other side.

NUGGET ONE

Saints, only Mark's account mentions that "other *little* ships" followed them. Imagine, Saints, these were people who heard Jesus' teaching and preaching and could not get enough and followed Him in their *"little ships!"*

These people were about to witness an extroadinary miracle which would change their very lives. Had their ships not come in, they would have missed it, Saints!

Imagine those whose ships remained on the shore . . .

Saints, if you seek a miracle, you must cast your little ship in and follow Jesus! Has your little ship come in or is it still on the shore?

These little ships were caught amid a storm so great that water filled their ships "to the full." Imagine the fear that must have overwhelmed them! They must have been close to Jesus' ship because they sought more teaching from Him. All of them must have heard His disciples in terror for their lives too. They must have heard them say to Jesus, *"carest thou not that we perish?"* Wow. imagine the chaos! Each of them must have felt utter hopelessness. They certainly must have realized that in their "little ships" and powerless bodies they were defenseless against such a tempest.

But the text says,*"He arose!"* Jesus arose, Saints, and told the sea to *"be still."* That Greek word is *muzzle*. Jesus, in front of all who's ship came in, told this tempest to "muzzle it." What a lifesaving, extroadinary miracle that would have been missed had their little ships not come in!

NUGGET TWO

Saints, Jesus *"He arose"* another time and provided another miracle that snatched us from the very threshold of hell! But our "little ships" must come in and seek, trust, and surrender to Christ! Again I ask, "Has your ship come in?"

Next, only Mark mentions that during the tempest Jesus was asleep "on a pillow." Jesus was resting in the love of our Father God. Imagine Jesus' pillow must have been soggy from the water that filled the ship, and yet He remained comfortable in the perfect love of our Father God.

Have you ever been in such distress that, as David said, even his pillow was soaked from his tears? Have you been there, Saints? Remember, Jesus had obeyed our Father God by teaching and preaching until He was very tired. Jesus had fulfilled the will of God and Jesus was at sweet peace during the storm.

You, too, can have such sweet peace that you can rest during your stormy trials because our Father has thoughts and a desire for peace for His children. However, your ship must come in and seek Jesus! Has your ship come in, my friends, or is your ship still on the shore?

Jeremiah 29:11 (KJV)
[11] *"For I know the thoughts that I think toward you, saith the LORD, thoughts of peace, and not of evil, to give you an expected end."*

God Bless!

NUGGETS TO LIVE BY

DRINKING FROM THE CUP OF SALVATION

Saints, as I found myself pondering over what happened at our church's last Easter service, I realized I had been led by the Spirit to do something I had never done before but always thought about doing. All churches experience an increase in numbers three holidays each year: Christmas, Mother's Day, and Easter. Those who know me have heard me refer to these Christians as C.M.E. Christians—that you really do not see them except these three times during the year . . . you know them!

Well, this Easter service the Spirit had me to call out and challenge these C.M.E. Christians this year to be more committed to God's purpose for their lives. After all, who would take a million-dollar check and put it in their desk drawer and bring it out three times a year and just look at it or see God as only an answer to their 9-1-1 calls?

Saints, the Spirit had me challenge these C.M.E. Christians to return the next week and really see the purpose of Easter in their lives. Praise God many returned, and the Spirit lead us to this Psalm:

Psalm 116:12-1–3 (KJV)

> [12] *"What shall I render unto the LORD for all his benefits toward me?*
> [13] *I will take the cup of salvation and call upon the name of the LORD."*

🏷 NUGGET ONE

Saints, when we consider all that our God has placed at our feet, how can we not drink from the cup of our salvation? How can we not praise Him continually and desire to be together with fellow brothers and sisters in worship daily? God did not create His people to be on an island alone or undercover in ministry.

When we ponder the facts of our God breathing life into our nostrils, creating the earth and all its animals and placing it at our feet, how can we only want to worship and praise Him just three times a year, or three times a day for that matter?

When we ponder the fact that our God created the sun to give us comfort by day and the moon to give us light by night and seasons to give us the riches of His glory, how can we only want to worship and praise Him just three times a year, or three times a day for that matter?

C.M.E. Christians, what can you "render unto the Lord for all His benefits toward you?"

🏷 NUGGET TWO

The greatest benefit toward all of us, the saved and unsaved, is the way of salvation made possible at the cross when Jesus said, "It is finished." The question is, "Will you take and drink from your cup of salvation offered to you by the blood of our redeemer?"

Taking and drinking from this cup involves more than just confessing a belief. It involves becoming a new creature "in Christ." By this our life changes from being all about self to all about Jesus Christ. This we do by taking up our cross and dying to self and living for Christ. C.M.E. Christians, what will you render for the benefit of your salvation? Paul puts it this way:

Galatians 2:20 (KJV)
20 "I am crucified with Christ: nevertheless I live; yet not I, but Christ liveth in me: and the life which I now live in the flesh I live by the faith of the Son of God, who loved me and gave himself for me."

Paul is talking about the zeal of complete surrender! Have you surrendered to our God through Jesus Christ completely or are you just rendering your "leftovers" of time and worship? Giving your best to your idols on the days you should give your "best" by being with fellow brothers and sisters in worship to our God who has offered you the benefits of taking and drinking from the cup of salvation?

Saints, next time I will probably not have another C.M.E. Christian attend services in our church again . . . kidding! However, if you think I am harsh, I leave you with what our Father says about those lukewarm C.M.E. Christians:

Revelation 3:15–16 (AMP)
15 "I know your [record of] works and what you are doing; you are neither cold nor hot. Would that you were cold or hot! 16 So, because you are lukewarm and neither cold nor hot, I will spew you out of My mouth!"

Saints, it can't get harsher than that! Let us call upon the name of the Lord!

God Bless!

DRAW ME NEARER, PRECIOUS LORD!
Psalm 51:11-19

Saints, have you ever felt distance between you and God? A distance that is so significant that you could do nothing but literally cry? Those tears then bringing you to your knees crying out in prayer to God? Knowing that this distance is due to you falling out of the center of God's will by your sin and knowing that God did not leave you, but your sin caused the distance between you and God? What would you do?

We will look at three things that David seeks as we close out this Psalm. We will see David ask for three things and then his prayer turns into promises!

NUGGET ONE

Saints, how many times when God answers your prayer do you promise God that you will do things such as attend church more regularly, devote more time in God's Word, never to be a slave to a certain sin anymore, or be more involved in your church in kingdom building? However, you find these promises lack the zeal and commitment once God has answered your prayer? If this is you, then this final part of the Psalm is your answer.

David asked God to not cast him out of His presence! Saints, the reason David asked this is because he knew that his sin deserved just that—to be cast out of God's presence! He also knew that there was no blood sacrifice that was available to him for his sins of murder and adultery. David did not want to be deprived of God's favor—a favor that he had been blessed with as a shepherd boy and now a king. David needed to be drawn nearer to God.

Saints, it is a horrible feeling to be in such a state, desperately seeking to be drawn nearer to our God!

Then David's prayer moved to asking that God not take His Spirit from him. Thank God this portion of David's prayer does not apply to us as God's children on this side of the cross. That is because as saved children of God, the Holy Spirit dwells within us to the day of redemption:

Ephesians 4:30 (KJV)
"And grieve not the Holy Spirit of God, whereby ye are sealed unto the day of redemption."

As Saints, we will never lose the Holy Spirit that dwells within us, but we can grieve Him, and as 1 Thessalonians also reminds us, we are able to quench the Holy Spirit as well.

NUGGET TWO

Saints, all praises to our Heavenly Father for sealing us with the Holy Spirit that is always working within our lives, leading us to be obedient to Him! However, while David's prayer does not apply to us today, we can grieve and quench the work of the Holy

Spirit by ignoring Him, disobeying Him, neglecting Him, and, yes, procrastinating in following His leading. Our prayer should be that we have a greater embrace of the work of the Holy Spirit which dwells within us.

Finally, David asked God to restore the joy of God's salvation. David wanted to once again be able to converse with God. Saints, it is awesome to be able to talk with God without the guilt of our sin hovering and hindering our prayer . . . amen!

My friends, what would you promise if God did all these things for you, saving you from yourself?

David moves now to his promises to God because of God saving him from himself.

First, David shows us that a truly grateful heart cannot keep it a secret! Jeremiah said that keeping God's Word inside was like *"fire shut up in his bones."*

NUGGET THREE

Saints, I am reminded of an Elder that is part of the services that we carry out at the Kansas City Union Mission for the homeless. His awesome testimony is of our Father delivering him from the bondage of drugs. Now his ministry is to tell those who are still in this horrible bondage of the promise of deliverance by the awesome grace of our God. If only they will trust Him! David knew that to keep God's deliverance to himself would be like fire shut up in his bones, and he promised not only to teach sinners God's ways, but to convert them. Saints, since being delivered, to how many souls have you taught God's ways? How many have you converted?

Then David said his mouth shall show forth God's praise! David was sold out on praising God! Saints, when we realize the awesome grace of God from daily saving us from ourselves by His wisdom and grace, we can't help but to shout! David's praises are in many of the Psalms we read today. Psalms that we sing as praise songs in many of our churches around the world. Psalms that we memorize that encourage us as we walk this Christian journey—like **Psalm 23**! Saints, will you leave a legacy of praise like David? We all certainly have much reason to leave such a legacy of praise!

Finally, David knew that there was no burnt offering that could be offered for murder and adultery. The only offering God would accept was a contrite heart full of gratitude, devotion, obedience, and self-denial! This is exactly what David offered for God saving him from himself.

David was so grateful and full of joy that he offered a humble sacrifice to the occasion of deliverance. That being a whole bullock! This was a symbol of total submission to God. Today we do not offer animals on the altar, but we can offer ourselves wholly and totally surrendering ourselves to God, as God has through His awesome grace of adoption wholly delivered us from ourselves! We must not forget by simply being hearers of the Word *but doers*! How many times do we forget what our God has done for us by not putting His Word to action by deeds we do in obedience as we walk this Christian journey?

I leave you with this Scripture, **James 1:25:**

"But whoso looketh into the perfect law of liberty, and continueth therein, he being not a forgetful hearer, but a doer of the work, this man shall be blessed in his deed."

God Bless!

DEPRESSED, ARE YOU?

Saints, if we are not careful, we all can be subject to depression that can come from many things. Certainly, with the condition of our country and its darkness one can easily slip into depression.

The Israelites found themselves in such a state being under Babylonian captivity. They were in such a state that things appeared hopeless from their perspective. Saints, have you ever been there? Or do you know anyone who has?

Well, Saints, our Father was watchful over the Israelites and is watchful over all His people even today. In Ezekiel 37 our Father gave the prophet Ezekiel an amazing vision—one that is relevant to all saints even today!

That vision, Saints, is often referred to the "valley of dry bones." In the vision, Ezekiel found God had taken him back and forth through this valley of dry bones. Imagine dried up carcasses everywhere he looked!

God had revealed to Ezekiel that He knew the condition of the Israelites, but He needed Ezekiel to deliver a message to them.

NUGGET ONE

Saints, imagine a church full of dry bones. A church that has given up on God. What message would you give them if you were the pastor? If that is too hard for you to answer, then what would be the message you would expect a God-called pastor to give to you?

God had shown Ezekiel that life can be put back into dead bones and, Saints, life can be put back into a dead church! Saints, our Father can give life to the hopeless! Saints, all he is waiting for is us to come to him . . .

NUGGET TWO

In **Ezekiel 37:4–6,** God commands Ezekiel to preach to the people with the dry bones to first "hear the Word of the Lord." Are you in a church full of dry bones? The question is, are they listening to the life-changing Word that God has given to the pastor to give to them? Or are they instead judging this pastor as preaching too long or the choir is not entertaining enough to bring them out of their depression? Saints, God said tell those dry bones to hear His Word! That is why many churches are full of dry bones seeking entertainment instead of God's life-giving Word! God said tell them to "HEAR GOD'S WORD!"

NUGGET THREE

In these same verses, Saints, God gives the medicine for dry-bones syndrome. He makes it clear that He alone is the Special Doctor! He says, *"I will cause breath to enter in you and ye shall live."* He also says He will *"put breath in you and ye shall live."* Saints, that breath is the Holy Spirit! God's prescription for dry-bones syndrome to come to life is the Holy Spirit!

Saints, have you truly accepted Christ? Then you are without excuse to be a part of a church where you are the problem being a dry bone among other dry bones! Hear God's Word and be a doer of His Word! Trust in the Spirit that is in you, and allow the same Spirit that raised Jesus from the dead to raise you from "dry-bones syndrome"!

NUGGET FOUR

Saints, why did our Father tell Ezekiel to tell us this? Look at the verses! He said so that when He brought life into the dry bones they would know that He is the Lord!

Ah, Saints, do you know the Lord? The question is: if you are depressed as a child of God, do you really know Him as your deliverer? Have you listened to His life-giving Word? Have you looked forward to His deliverance through the Holy Spirit who lives within you?

God in verse 9 tells Ezekiel to command the four winds: ***"O breath, and breathe upon these slain that they may live."***

Saints, do you want to live? Do you want to be alive in Jesus? Trust in God's Word, starting here our salvation:

Ephesians 2:5–6 (AMP)
⁵ "Even when we were dead (slain) by [our own] shortcomings and trespasses, He made us alive together in fellowship and in union with Christ; [He gave us the very life of Christ Himself, the same new life with which He quickened Him, for] it is by grace (His favor and mercy which you did not deserve) that you are saved (delivered from judgment and made partakers of Christ's salvation).
⁶ And He raised us up together with Him and made us sit down together [giving us joint seating with Him] in the

heavenly sphere [by virtue of our being] in Christ Jesus (the Messiah, the Anointed One)."

God Bless!

BEING PREPARED FOR SATAN'S ATTACKS

Saints, in the tenth chapter of Daniel, we see a man "sold out" for God in his prayer! We see Daniel's heart aching regarding his people once being freed held from finishing the temple in their homeland.

This was crucial as in the Old Testament where there existed the belief that God was in the temple. Well, today we know that our God is with us:

> **John 14:23 (KJV)**
> *"Jesus answered and said unto him, 'If a man love me, he will keep my words: and my Father will love him, and we will come unto him, and make our abode with him.'"*

NUGGET ONE

Saints, when Daniel realized this travesty, he had many choices of retaliation. He could have gone to the leaders whom he worked for as an interpreter of dreams to fight for the Israelites rights to build the temple. Instead he went to God. How many times do we as Christians today go to man, the Supreme Court or some other refuge seeking man's help? Claiming religious liberty and freedom . . .

David realized that we do not war against flesh and blood but against principalities, powers, and rulers of darkness:

Ephesians 6:12 (KJV)
"For we wrestle not against flesh and blood, but against principalities, against powers, against the rulers of the darkness of this world, against spiritual wickedness in high places."

Saints, more importantly, Daniel realized that the Angels, Gabriel and Michael, were already fighting on their behalf. Daniel had called upon the Lord in deep prayer, sacrificing himself and the pleasures of his flesh for others rather than himself. He gave up meat, wine, and anointing himself with oil for God to hear his prayer and answer him.

NUGGET TWO

Saints, how many times when we are praying does our flesh hinder our prayer? Perhaps hunger strikes and you shorten your prayer, or Satan flashed a picture in your mind that should not be there, or Satan tells you that you are too tired to pray and you will do it later. Daniel chastened himself by denying his flesh and putting it under his control and went to the Lord. Oh, what an awesome picture of one sold out for God! Saints, how many times have you done this? Sacrificed self by chastening your flesh and praying for someone other than yourself?

David did this for three weeks! Many Saints today can't or won't sacrifice and chasten their flesh for three hours. Makes one ponder . . .

Remember the Western Wagon Train? When danger came upon them they would circle the wagons to protect each other in battle. Wouldn't it be awesome if we would circle our wagons in prayer for one another? Each covering the backs of the other? My friends that is being sold out for our God!

The text further says that after three weeks of prayer, Daniel was walking by a great river and looked up and saw the Lord. What an awesome sight to see Jesus! (Yes, it was Jesus—the same description of Jesus is in **Rev. 1:12–17.**) It was so overwhelming that Daniel fell to the ground in awe of the glory of Jesus! Saints, have you ever had Jesus reveal himself to you during your trials? When this happens, you are certain He has answered your prayers and that causes you great humility and inability to speak. Sometimes all you can get to come out of your mouth with the greatest admiration is "Thank you, Jesus!"

Daniel was there, Saints, and the Angel Gabriel had to touch Daniel and pick him up and sit him on his hands and knees.

NUGGET THREE

Saints, look at verses 12 and 13 of our text in Daniel. Gabriel gave Daniel an awesome message that we all should be reminded of even today. Gabriel confirmed to Daniel that God had heard his prayer from the first day. He also recognized Daniel for "setting his heart to understand" before God and "chastening himself" before God. Saints, our God recognizes those that are sold out for Him! Are you?

Then he tells Daniel something that we all should be reminded of as we walk this Christian journey today. He tells Daniel that he was delayed because he was fighting the demons already on Daniel's behalf!

Saints, how many times we think God is slow to answer our prayers and we begin fighting flesh and blood. Instead of being patient and trusting that God is already fighting on our behalf before we say, "Amen."

When Daniel realized that Angels had already been dispatched, God's Word says that he fell "dumb" (unable to speak)!

Saints, what are you praying for that God has already dispatched Angels on your behalf? Have you set your heart to understanding and chastened your flesh before God? Are you sold out in your prayer? One of the greatest "ifs" Jesus said:

John 15:7 (KJV)
"If ye abide in me, and my words abide in you, ye shall ask what ye will, and it shall be done unto you."

God Bless!

ARE YOU MAKING A DEAL WITH THE DEVIL?

Saints, do any of you remember taking math tests in high school? Do you remember those math problems where you gave the answer without going through the steps revealing how you arrived at it? I remember my teacher would always mark my answer in red as wrong even though the answer was correct.

That always troubled me as I thought it ridiculous to take time from finishing the test to go through the steps and not be able to complete the other problems.

Saints, I now realize in my much more mature age that my teacher was teaching me the importance of linear thought as well as a Spiritual lesson. I wonder if she was even aware of the latter?

NUGGET ONE

Saints, how many times in our Spiritual walk do we make decisions in haste that we feel are accurate without God? Without seeking God's guidance? Without standing on His promises to protect us?

Saints, thus finding ourselves in a dilemma because we decided in haste. Even making a deal with the Devil! Knowing more than God!

Well, Saints, you were not alone! Isaiah gave a message from God to the Israelites that they in haste made a covenant with death and hell. A covenant that was made with unbelievers that had even lied to them. Seeking the protection of unbelievers when God had a covenant to protect them!

Isaiah 28:14–15 (KJV)
[14] "Wherefore hear the Word of the LORD, ye scornful men, that rule this people which is in Jerusalem. [15] Because ye have said, 'We have made a covenant with death, and with hell are we at agreement; when the overflowing scourge shall pass through, it shall not come unto us: for we have made lies our refuge, and under falsehood have we hid ourselves . . .'"

NUGGET TWO

Ah, Saints, the very next word is like music of deliverance to our hearts! This word is the love of our Father to us even today, *"therefore"*! It is a word symbolizing our Father to the rescue of His hard-headed children . . . *us*!

Our Father said, **"I lay in Zion for a foundation a stone, a tried stone, a precious stone, a sure foundation: he that believeth shall not make haste."** Yes, Saints, He is referencing the church but also our hearts.

Who is this stone? Saints, it is Jesus Christ, His only begotten Son! Look with me at His résumé!

A tried stone! Jesus would defeat the world for them and has already defeated the world for us at the cross, where He prepared a way of deliverance for our souls! Oh yes, He had taken on the world and defeated Satan! Christ our foundation is tried, tested and guaranteed!

> ### Isaiah 26:3–4 (KJV)
> *³ "Thou wilt keep him in perfect peace, whose mind is stayed on thee: because he trusteth in thee. ⁴ Trust ye in the LORD for ever: for in the LORD JEHOVAH is everlasting strength . . ."*

A precious cornerstone! The cornerstone was usually thirty-eight feet long and one hundred tons! Saints, this symbolizes the unlimited power and strength of our Messiah! Without this stone the building would collapse and without this stone our lives and churches will collapse! For His power and grace towards us and the church is new every morning and sufficient for that day. No need to make haste, Saints!

> ### Psalm 37:7 (KJV)
> *⁷ "Rest in the LORD, and wait patiently for him: fret not thyself . . ."*

A sure foundation! Saints, our Savior is secure enough to build our church upon and secure enough to build our lives upon! Daily we are to build upon this foundation by faith and trust in Jesus. Standing sure and secure upon this faith through the trials of this life.

Charles H. Spurgeon puts it this way, "For how canst thou know that thou haste faith until thy faith is exercised? Real growth in grace is the result of sanctified trials!"

God Bless!

A TRANSFORMED WOMAN

Saints, as we look through the Bible, we can see many men who have made a mark in their walk of faith. Many women have made this journey as well. However, this one has made such a significant transformation that she has been listed in Matthew chapter 1 as part of the generation of Christ!

NUGGET ONE

Saints, we all have family and friends who have "stiff necks," or as my grandmother use to say, "hard heads." We would bet the farm that no one could ever change them! Truth be told, many of us could simply look in the mirror and know that is not true, because if our God could change us, Uncle so-and-so is a cake walk!

In Joshua chapter 2. we see a harlot named Rahab be transformed into a woman of God. How did this happen? *Read on!* Can this happen today? *Absolutely!*

Rahab in the midst of the fear of her people and family recognized God as the God of Heaven and Earth.

Joshua 2:11 (KJV)
[11] "And as soon as we had heard these things, our hearts did melt, neither did there remain any more courage in any man, because of you: for the LORD your God, he is God in heaven above, and in earth beneath."

Saints, Rahab, a harlot, knew where the Israelites received their strength and victories from. How many of you know where your strength and victories come from? Rahab sought deliverance from God as she recognized God both of Heaven and eEarth amid her fear. When our backs are against the wall, do we take the time to look to Heaven for our strength here on Earth?

Not only did Rahab seek deliverance for herself but also her family.

NUGGET TWO

Imagine Rahab convincing her family to trust God by convincing them to stay in her house when the Israelites came to take the city. Imagine Rahab convincing them to trust that they would be spared by the very God that she now recognized as Lord and they did not. What a picture of evangelism!

Saints, as we walk by faith, are we seeking others that are unbelievers to join us in doing the same? Are we convincing family members to trust in God, especially when their backs are against the wall? Or are we oblivious to the true meaning of our deliverance:

Matthew 7:16–20 (KJV)
[16] "Ye shall know them by their fruits. Do men gather grapes of thorns, or figs of thistles?

> *[17] Even so every good tree bringeth forth good fruit; but a corrupt tree bringeth forth evil fruit.*
> *[18] A good tree cannot bring forth evil fruit, neither can a corrupt tree bring forth good fruit.*
> *[19] Every tree that bringeth not forth good fruit is hewn down and cast into the fire. 20 Wherefore by their fruits ye shall know them."*

Rahab, a harlot, brought forth good fruit as she convinced her family to trust God for deliverance. As a result, she became part of the generation of Christ! She became attached to the True Vine, Jesus Christ. What an awesome woman that led her family to Christ during the storm!

Are you going through a storm today? Is an unbeliever in your family going through a storm with their backs against the wall? They too can receive deliverance by becoming a part of the family of Christ. They too can become sons of God and be strangers to this world—a world that will no longer know them because it does not know Christ.

I leave you with this Scripture:

1 John 3:1–2 (KJV)

> *[1] "Behold, what manner of love the Father hath bestowed upon us that we should be called the sons of God: therefore the world knoweth us not, because it knew him not. [2] Beloved, now are we the sons of God, and it doth not yet appear what we shall be: but we know that, when he shall appear, we shall be like him; for we shall see him as he is."*

If you want deliverance, trust in God through the blood of Jesus Christ!
God Bless!

A MATTER OF THE HEART

S aints, as we continue to explore the topic of what being "sold out" for the Lord looks like, we must take a moment to look at Joshua. Joshua was truly sold out for our Lord! Joshua had walked with the Lord through many trials and battles. As a result, Joshua came to realize that the Lord had never failed him.

Today, Saints, if we would take a little soul-searching inventory, we too would realize that our Lord has never failed us either. Our friends, family, and even self would fail us but NOT our Lord! Especially when we agree with our Lord and walk with Him.

NUGGET ONE

Amos 3:3 (KJV)
³ *"Can two walk together, except they be agreed?"*

Saints, how can we walk with the Lord and not agree with Him? Impossible! Joshua, throughout the book of Joshua, gave prophetic messages to the people. However, we need to focus on the message given by him in **chapter 24:14–24** to get a picture of what being sold out for our Lord looks like.

This final message from Joshua was from his heart that was sold out for God. From his heart, Joshua gave an invitation to the people to choose who they walk for and with. Would it be false gods or our God? This message is very important to us even today.

Saints, will we continue to follow the gods of this world, the lust of the flesh, eyes and the pride of life?

1 John 2:15–17 (KJV)

^{15}"Love not the world, neither the things that are in the world. If any man loveloves the world, the love of the Father is not in him. ^{16}For all that is in the world, the lust of the flesh, and the lust of the eyes, and the pride of life, is not of the Father, but is of the world. ^{17}And the world passeth away, and the lust thereof: but he that doeth the will of God abideth for ever."

The gods of this world are not of God, nor does it allow us to walk with our Lord. Joshua was warning the Israelites and now us as Christians that we cannot be sold out for God and remain slaves to this world. We must agree with our Lord and obey Him in order to walk with Him. This is what being sold out looks like!

NUGGET TWO

The Israelites recognized how the Lord had delivered them through many obstacles and won all their battles against armies whose goal was to destroy them, yet the Lord remained true to His promise.

Sound familiar, Saints? How many trials that should have defeated us did God instead deliver us? How many obstacles did our Lord move out of our way as we traveled the road He prepared for us to travel? Yet we fail to stay on this road through our disobedience! *Been there, Saints?*

Joshua said in his invitation for us to choose "TODAY"! Choose today who we will serve! No time to be "LUKEWARM" for the Lord! No time to give glory to our will while simultaneously attempting to give glory to our Lord's will!

That is why Joshua **(24:19)** dared the Israelites by saying they could not serve the Lord. In other words, they could not be sold out for God and serve two wills.

Serving God at one hundred percent is the only answer! Ninety-nine and a half percent won't do! Joshua was speaking from the heart.

NUGGET THREE

Saints, we need to be like Joshua and tell those in our churches that they cannot serve two masters. Too many times we ignore letting the children of our God play church at ninety-nine and a half percent! When Joshua finally allowed them to confess that they would serve God for all He had done for them, he reminded them that they must hold each other accountable. How can you hold someone accountable if you are not sold out for God?

Joshua was a true leader, sold out for our Lord when he told the Israelites that:

Joshua 24:15 (KJV)

¹⁵ "And if it seems evil unto you to serve the LORD, choose you this day whom ye will serve; whether the gods which your fathers served that were on the other side of the flood, or the gods of the Amorites, in whose land ye dwell: but as for me and my house, we will serve the LORD."

Saints, are you prepared to lead "lukewarm" saints to a more sold out heart for the Lord? It begins with your example! Are YOU SOLD OUT for our Lord?

Psalm 116:12–13 (KJV)
[12] "What shall I render unto the LORD for all his benefits toward me? [13] I will take the cup of salvation and call upon the name of the LORD."

God Bless!

ARE YOU THE APPLE OF OUR GOD'S EYE?

Saints, do you ever find yourself being falsely accused by this world? Have you ever felt you were alone against the world? Well, David found himself in such a situation. This situation was so devastating that it drove him to pray prostrate before God.

This prayer can be found in **Psalm 17**:

Psalm 17:8 (KJV)
⁸ "Keep me as the apple of the eye, hide me under the shadow of thy wings . . ."

The Amplified Bible says it this way:

Psalm 17:8 (AMP)
⁸ "Keep and guard me as the pupil of Your eye; hide me in the shadow of Your wings . . ."

David longed for the protection that could only come from God!

🏷 NUGGET ONE

Saints, the pupil is a powerful part of the eye, yet the weakest. The pupil in its weakness stands in need of protection from the evil of this world. The pupil is surrounded by a socket of bone which is a fortress for the pupil. It is also covered by the eyebrow which guards it from the bitter sweat of the forehead. That is the hedge of protection our Lord gives us as believers.

The eyelashes strain dust, wind, and dirt from getting to the pupil. This represents our Lord's shield of protection which fights our battles. Saints, the eyelids are the curtains of the eye that open to allow the pupil to see the wondrous works of God and close to allow peaceful sleep away from the world and its distractions.

What an awesome request made by David! Even though he was strong, he was yet weak! But God reminds us that in our weakness, He is strong! Praise God that we as believers washed in the blood of His son Jesus Christ are standing as the "apple of God's eye"!

🏷 NUGGET TWO

Saints, we must not overlook a crucial point. Our Father's Word reminds us that as a church we are to function as the body.

1 Corinthians 12:12 (KJV)
12 "For as the body is one, and hath many members, and all the members of that one body, being many, are one body: so also is Christ."

Saints, to be the "apple of God's eye," we must as a church represent the body of Christ. As church members we are a part of something bigger than who we are individually. We must love, protect, encourage, and support one another as the eyebrows, eyelashes, eye sockets, and eyelids. As a church, we are a family! We laugh, cry, excel, pray, forgive, and worship together as a family dependent on each other. We are *FAMILY*—a *FAMILY OF GOD*!

Ecclesiastes 4:9–10 (KJV)
⁹ "Two are better than one; because they have a good reward for their labour.
¹⁰ For if they fall, the one will lift up his fellow: but woe to him that is alone when he falleth; for he hath not another to help him up."

Are you the *"apple of God's eye"*? Are you the *"apple of God's eye"* in your church?

God Bless!

ARE YOU "SUCH A MAN"?

Saints, "such a man" is referenced by Jesus Christ in the book of **Matthew 26:18.** Jesus, after being asked by His Disciples where they were to eat the Passover meal, replied, "Go into the city to such a man . . ."

Who was this man and what did he witness? Some believe he was a man who believed in Jesus but was afraid to admit it for fear of being kicked out of the synagogue. While others believe that his name is not mentioned for fear of Judas after hearing it and his location would share this information to those seeking to kill Jesus.

However, Saints, I believe that "such a man" has no name that we may see if we can insert our name in this person. Think about his attributes first, Sints.

NUGGET ONE

Jesus gave us clues about "such a man." The first clue was that he must have known Jesus as *Master*, as Jesus told the Disciples to say to him, ***"Master saith."*** Saints, do you know Jesus as your Master? Do you have a relationship with him that you would recognize His calling out to you? Are you "such a man"?

🔖 NUGGET TWO

The second clue—Jesus also said to tell "such a man" His "time had come." This man had to have understood this meaning and its relevance to the cross and the pending New Covenant in the blood of Our Savior!

Saints, on this side of the cross, do you fully understand the awesome relevance of the powerful blood of Jesus? Do you understand that He replaced the Passover at the house of "such a man"? Replacing it with a New Covenant in His Blood by the remission of our sin for all eternity. That He died once for all never to die again! Saints, do you know this? Does your life reflect this knowledge? Are you "such a man"?

🔖 NUGGET THREE

The third clue is that Jesus told the disciples to tell "such a man" that they were going to "keep the Passover at (his) house." Notice Jesus did not ask whether He could but that He would! Jesus knew the heart of "such a man." Jesus knows our hearts too. The question, Saints, is . . . can Jesus depend on your hearts? Have you opened your house to receive the New Covenant? Have you opened your heart to receive the New Covenant that Christ shed His blood for you? Saints, "such a man" opened his house to the Master! Are you "such a man"?

Imagine what "such a man" must have witnessed in his house that day. First, when Jesus took the bread in His hands declaring that it was His body broken for them. Imagine, Saints, that bread resting in His hands a picture of His control and desire to voluntarily be offered for our sins! Up until then the Passover denoted the pain the Israelites experienced for God, but now Jesus had shown agape love and grace by taking on pain for them as well as us in a New Covenant! Imagine "such a man" witnessing this! Saints, have you truly embraced the significance of the Lord's Supper in your church, or are you going through the motions? Are you "such a man"?

Imagine "such a man" witnessing Jesus taking the cup in His hands, as well denoting the same desire to voluntarily go to the cross for us as He did when He took the bread. Now He says, "This is my blood of the New Testament, which is shed for many for the remission of sins." Wow, imagine "such a man" witnessing Jesus testifying that He is the Messiah, the Lamb of God Isaiah prophesied about! That by His stripes we are healed! That He will die once that all who believe would be saved!

Jesus further told the disciples to "drink all of it." Imagine the goosebumps "such a man" must have experienced then. Jesus was letting him and the disciples know that to be delivered, they had to fully embrace what Jesus was about to do and to fully embrace the power of His blood to deliver man once and for all!

Saints, have you truly embraced the power of the blood of Jesus Christ? Have you truly embraced the work of Calvary? Are you "such a man"? Or do you doubt your salvation? Do you believe that you can lose your salvation when you never earned it in the first place? Are you "such a man"?

Ephesians 1:6–7 (KJV)
⁶ "To the praise of the glory of his grace, wherein he hath made us accepted in the beloved. ⁷ In whom we have redemption through his blood, the forgiveness of sins, according to the riches of his grace . . ."

God Bless!

NUGGETS TO LIVE BY

A LOVE LETTER IN TROUBLED TIMES

Saints, more than ever we are witnessing troubled times for our nation. Overt murders of unarmed citizens without remorse by those that are to protect and serve and blatant callous retaliation by citizens that have lost tolerance for this evil perpetrated against them. Not to mention our justice system refusing to take a stand to abate further debauchery from BOTH sides.

In 2017, the killing of police was up 44 percent to 26 percent, while *Huffington Post* reported that 136 blacks were killed by police in 2016. Somewhere around 580 unarmed white and black citizens were shot by police as well.

As if this is not enough, there has been 188 school shootings since 2013 and an estimate of 780,000 same sex marriages have taken place since it has been legalized. Abortions are down but remaining at approximately 1.1 million per year!

Saints, anyone of you doubt that Satan is on his job?

Ah, but our God has sent us a love letter to consider in these troubled times!

God first gave this message to the Israelites before they were to enter Canaan. Their troubled times were yet to come, and He wanted to prepare them with these words:

Deuteronomy 7:9 (KJV)
⁹"Know therefore that the LORD thy God, he is God, the faithful God, which keepeth covenant and mercy with them that love him and keep his commandments to a thousand generations..."

NUGGET ONE

Saints, God reminded them as well as us today to KNOW THY GOD, HE IS GOD even in trouble times! That word *know* in the Hebrew is "YADA" which means to have a relationship with Him and confess and profess that relationship verbally and in our actions. God is telling us to remember that He is still our God, and we are to know and make this known in good times as well as bad times. That no matter the circumstances today or yet to come, God is still in control! Be not discouraged because He alone is God!

NUGGET TWO

God says: "THE FAITHFUL GOD"! In their pending trouble, God is yet faithful! The Israelites should remember this as God had brought them a mighty long way. He has also brought each of us a mighty long way.

But more importantly, that word *faithful* means "AMAN"— that our God will build us up and support us in troubled times while remaining true to His Word. Look at how Paul gives this message of love from God to the Thessalonians:

> **2 Thessalonians 3:3 (AMP)**
> *³ "Yet the Lord is faithful, and He will strengthen [you] and set you on a firm foundation and guard you from the evil [one]."*

Yes, Saints, in troubled times our God is "AMAN," our strength and foundation. We must remember this during these times and profess Him to this nation and to our fellow citizens. Satan will try to use these times to divide us and cause us as Christians to become discouraged and take the evil way over God's way of love for one another.

Once we embrace God as "AMAN," our FAITHFUL GOD, our strength and foundation alone, we will understand the last part of His love letter to us in troubled times:

> *"(God) keepeth covenant and mercy with them that love him and keep his commandments to a thousand generations . . ."*

God will keep His Word, Saints, and will have mercy with them that love Him and reveal this by being obedient to Him! Let us pray for our nation as we profess Christ:

> *2 Chronicles 7:14 (AMP)*
> *¹⁴ "If My people, who are called by My name, shall humble themselves, pray, seek, crave, and require of necessity My face and turn from their wicked ways, then will I hear from heaven, forgive their sin, and heal their land."*

God Bless!

NUGGETS TO LIVE BY

A BRIGHT AND SHINING STAR FOR MY LORD

Saints, do you want to be a bright and shining star for our Lord? Well, the Mission Ministry of our National Baptist Convention has a pledge that they repeat at the end of their weekly meeting. The pledge ends:

I pledge to devote myself and seek divine aid and guidance daily that I might become a living witness and a bright and shining light for my Lord!

In the Old Testament, Daniel gave a prophesy about those who would do just that:

Daniel 12:3 (AMP)
³ "And the teachers and those who are wise shall shine like the brightness of the firmament, and those who turn many to righteousness (to uprightness and right standing with God) [shall give forth light] like the stars forever and ever."

🪙 NUGGET ONE

Saints, those that are wise in the Spirit of the Lord and by the Spirit seek the lost and turn them to Christ, placing them in right standing with God are likened to bright and shining stars for our Lord!

Notice Daniel says, "forever and ever." Saints, that brightness will shine all the way to the Bema Seat of God where those who win souls for Christ will receive their Crown of Rejoicing! Those that help to populate Heaven!

James puts it this way:

James 5:19–20 (KJV)
[19] "Brethren, if any of you do err from the truth,
and one convert him;
[20] Let him know, that he which converteth the sinner
from the error of his way shall save a soul from death
and shall hide a multitude of sins."

Saints, are you truly ready to be a bright and shining star for our Lord? Have you experienced the soul-enlightening joy of winning souls for Christ? How many did you win, say, last week? Last month? Last year?

If you say zero, then certainly you have had lost souls cross your path who were in need of the realization of the blessing of Jesus Christ and His gift of salvation . . . surely? What did you do? Did you become an "undercover Christian," keeping silent? Afraid to be accused of "judging"? Afraid of rejection and ridicule by even friends, coworkers, and even family?

🟦 NUGGET THREE

Saints, Paul mentions the joy he had for the Saints in the Thessalonian church. They, by faith, labored in love seeking those who were lost. Saints, that word *labor* means "in pain," such as a woman in childbirth. These Saints were grieved, ridiculed, and tortured by religionist and fellow Gentiles and family for spreading the gGospel of Jesus Christ. In all this they stayed the course. They shed their blood for the cause of Christ!

Saints, can you imagine if this world had Christians like that during these dark times? None of us have shed an ounce of blood for the cause of Christ, yet they did. Why are today's Saints such "Undercover Christians" that they cannot even count the number of lost souls that they have shared the awesome Gospel Message with?

But they will look to man and man's laws to do what God has directed them to do! Even though God has equipped them to do this by giving them His Spirit to guide them. If only they would "step out in faith" and seek the lost with this sweet, soul-saving message. After all, God died for them too.

Those who convert lost sinners give forth the light as shining stars! Those who are undercover Christians place their light under their coats! Saints, the Crown of rRejoicing is an awesome Crown, but many I'm afraid will miss it, yet are equipped to receive it. Is that you? Will you receive this Crown? Therefore, Paul said this about the Thessalonian Church:

1 Thessalonians 2:19–20 (KJV)
[19] "For what is our hope, or joy, or crown of rejoicing? Are not even ye in the presence of our Lord Jesus Christ at his coming? [20] For ye are our glory and joy."

God Bless!

NUGGETS TO LIVE BY

. . . BECAUSE HE FIRST LOVED ME (PART I)
1 John 4:7-11

How many of you really love God? How many of you really know that God *is* love? How many of you know that His very nature *is* love? If your answer is a resounding "AMEN" to these questions, then please allow me to assume that you are born again, and if so **Philippians 2:1–4** demands that we, *". . . be like minded, having the same love . . ."* and abundantly much more!

In other words, a born-again Christian that claims to love God must be a loving, lovable person. Wow! We can just stay there for a moment and meditate. Imagine if all those who claim they love God would in fact have taken on His nature and became lovable, loving creatures . . .

What a wonderful world it would be! It would be as they say, "a slice of heaven." However, we know that this currently is quite the opposite, but it is possible. Look at our text in 1 John. As born-again Christians there are two P's to consider.

The first P is POWER: As Christians if we are truly under the **POWER** of God by surrendering our life to Him, we are empowered by Him to love. We love by His power and not by our own feeble power. As man loves darkness more than light.

The second P is PRODUCT: As Christians we must remember that we are the **PRODUCT** of God's grace. God's grace that snatched us out of the very condemnation we richly deserved. That being hell itself.

NUGGET ONE

As Christians, sometimes it is tough to love those who are unlovable. Being from Chicago, I use to say that sometimes you want to walk someone down a Chicago alley . . . two walk in, and one comes out! Now I say we both come out stronger than before we went in . . . Amen! Why? Because I am now under the POWER of God and the PRODUCT of His grace! It is all about Him and no longer about me! As God's children we are all called to imitate Christ, who is love. **John 15:12** says:

"This is my commandment, That ye love one another, as I have loved you."

However, I hear someone saying, "Pastor, in this dark world that we live in where people curse God, deny God, rebel against God, disobey and reject God, how does one know that God is love? Saints, how would you answer this question?

Revelation 3:20 is the answer!
"Behold, I stand at the door, and knock: if any man hear my voice, and opens the door, I will come in to him, and will sup with him, and he with me."

God's most important demonstration of the fact that He is love in this dark world is His plan of salvation. A plan that will bring man back into fellowship with Him for eternity through the sacrifice of His son! His love for all mankind is standing at the very door of the heart of man. Standing there waiting for man to open the door of His spiritually bankrupt heart that he may sup with Him and nourish man to spiritual health and redemption.

God's love is not destruction and tearing down of man but building up and caring for man. Man is important to God and God did not "pick and choose" which man, for His son came that all men might be saved!

1 Timothy 2:3–6
"For this is good and acceptable in the sight of God our Saviour; Who will have all men to be saved, and to come unto the knowledge of the truth. For there is one God, and one mediator between God and men, the man Christ Jesus; 6 Who gave himself a ransom for all, to be testified in due time."

Psalm 107:2 says let the redeemed of the Lord say so! Saints, we are called to love all men even those who are unlovable. If we are truly redeemed, we should show our love by saying so. Not just in words but in action. This text is not just saying by your lips only, but by your actions. After all, there is a lot of truth to "actions speaking louder than words."

Saints, again God demonstrated that He is love by sacrificing His son on the cross and His son to this day stands at the door of every man's spiritually bankrupted heart. Then why would any man refuse to sacrifice himself to God and open the door?

The world is dark not because there is a faction of people thinking that God is not love; instead there are a faction of people not wanting to accept God as love. That is why we as Christians are to love all men as God demonstrates to reveal to man a better way! A way of love . . .

John reminds us of this in verse 11 by saying, "Beloved, if God so loved us, we ought also to love one another"

NUGGET TWO

Saints, we must love because God is love and He first loved us. This is our responsibility and commandment until the return of Jesus Christ. Our love for one another will present us holy and without blame at that time. After all, if one does not love he will be held accountable for his lack of obedience when Jesus returns. But remember the two P's! We can only do it by surrendering to God's POWER and remembering that we are the PRODUCT of His grace!

I leave you with God's Word . . .

1 Thessalonians 3:12–13

"And the Lord make you to increase and abound in love one toward another, and toward all men, even as we do toward you: To the end he may stablish your hearts unblameable in holiness before God, even our Father, at the coming of our Lord Jesus Christ with all his saints."

God Bless!

. . . BECAUSE HE FIRST LOVED ME (PART 2)
1 John 4:7-12, 21

The Power Within

Saints, how does one see or know that our God is love? The text emphasizes that no one has ever seen God at any time, in spite of all the hype we see on talk shows and in books—people foolishly claiming to have gone to heaven and come miraculously back to tell us about it. Cashing in on "filthy lucre" regarding this nonsense.

Jesus himself in **John 1:18** also confirmed, *"No man hath seen God at any time . . ."* Hence, run and take all your books back! Turn off those TV talk shows! *Listen to Jesus!*

I always stress that when I go to heaven I will not even desire to return to this life but wait for those who will be joining me . . . Amen!

So how does one see or know that our God is love? The answer is through His children! When we as His children accepted Christ as our Savior, God gave us His nature of love by placing His Spirit within us! In other words, the Holy Spirit that now dwells within the believer . . ." The Power Within!

Ephesians 1:13–14

"In whom ye also trusted, after that ye heard the Word of truth, the gospel of your salvation: in whom also after that ye believed, ye were sealed with that Holy Spirit of promise, which is the earnest of our inheritance until the redemption of the purchased possession, unto the praise of his glory."

God's own Spirit comes and lives within the believer after he has trusted the Gospel of His salvation and as a result given his life to Christ! Then God gives the believer this power to reflect His love to the lost as well as their Christian brothers.

This same Spirit safeguards and secures our salvation, Those who are truly saved are without excuse as God's Spirit will convict and stir the believer to obey God's commandment to reflect His nature of love by loving one another. All of us have fallen off track during our walk with the Lord at some time or another. However, it is this "power within" that stirs us to get back on track . . . Amen!

This coaxing from the Spirit reassures the believer that he is saved. It also reveals to the world that God is in fact love as demonstrated by the obedience of His children to love as He loves. The Spirit or "power within" gives the believer power to love because man in and of himself does not have the power to love as God requires! Nor can he.

Romans 8:7

"Because the carnal mind is enmity against God: for it is not subject to the law of God, neither indeed can be."

Therefore, if those who profess a belief in Jesus Christ do not have this "power within" to love, then the question becomes, are they truly saved? Either they think they can ignore the Spirit of God within them or they never really had the Spirit planted in them at all. They lack a true sincere conversion.

The Ephesians text above makes it clear that the true convert is "sealed," meaning that they are truly validated as God's purchased possession through their confession of belief in Jesus Christ. This confession acknowledges that the new believer has surrendered himself to the leading of the Holy Spirit in continued obedience to God. Hence, the obedience of the commandment to reflect God's love in this world by the "power within."

Romans 8:14
"For as many as are led by the Spirit of God, they are the sons of God."

When we reflect that God is love in this world, we can boldly go to the throne of judgment with our heads high because as God is love, so are we in this world.

Saints, sadly there will be professed Christians who refuse to love and will be afraid and tormented at the return of Jesus Christ and His angels! Those professed Christians, holding onto grudges, ignoring the needs of the poor, refusing to forgive and refusing to love the unlovable will be tormented by the thought of the return of Jesus Christ.

NUGGET ONE

Only perfect gGodly love, driven by the "power within" casts out this fear and torment.

After all, it is easy to love those who love you but even doing that without the "power within" is carnal and conditional. Just let the one who they love make a mistake, then that conditional love swiftly disappears and loathing replaces it!

When we stand boldly before a Holy God, reassured that we loved in this world as He is love, then His love has been perfected in us . . . halleluiah!

NUGGET TWO

Saints, God is love because He first loved us! Let us reveal this fact to the world by following the direction of God's nature. His Holy Spirit, the "power within" that we may stand boldly at the return of Jesus Christ!

I leave you with God's Word

1 John 5:17–19:

"Herein is our love made perfect, that we may have boldness in the day of judgment: because as he is, so are we in this world. 18 There is no fear in love; but perfect love casteth out fear: because fear hath torment. He that feareth is not made perfect in love. 19 We love him, because he first loved us."

God Bless!

AVOIDING A LIFE OF CHAOS

Friends, do you sometimes find yourselves in a very chaotic life, a life that seems to have no direction or no meaning? Do you yearn to know how the chaos you are going through will end? Will you survive it, or will it defeat you? Are you looking for direction through the chaos?

Well the answer my friend is in Jesus!

John 8:12 (KJV)
"Then spake Jesus again unto them, saying, 'I am the light of the world: he that followeth me shall not walk in darkness, but shall have the light of life.'"

NUGGET ONE

Friends no one can see the future nor the real meaning of life. Life's importance and significance is not revealed to man without Christ. Christ is the light of the world that reveals this world to man. Jesus is the light of men, meaning those who accept Him will have His light within them. His light that will guide man away from darkness!

Jesus as the light reveals to His believers the meaning of life and its purpose. After all, Jesus' very nature is light. As **1 John 1:5** reassures us that God is light and in Him there is no darkness!. Jesus, according to **Colossians 1:15,** instructs us that He is the very image of the invisible God. There is not a speck of darkness or blindness in Jesus.

While Jesus' light reveals that He is holy, righteous, and pure it also reveals "clearly the nature, the meaning, and destiny of all things."

NUGGET TWO

Friends, when the light of Jesus shines, it reveals the truth about man, the world, and about our God. If you are looking for clarity and answers, my friends, turn to Jesus because His light also reveals His love and care for us. His light also reveals His desire to love and care for the unbeliever if only that one would trust Jesus with his life.

Jesus' light also guides man. Imagine being in a burning building. Flames of life surrounding you as all you own is crumbling under the flames. Smoke and darkness permeate your path and you see no way out. You trip, stumble, and gasp for life-giving air, reaching and calling out for help. Then you look up and see a glimmer of light! You seek this light and follow it and suddenly the closer you get the clearer the path . . .

My friends, that is how spiritually our Savior makes clear the path of life if only man will accept Him! God will provide mercy to that man when that man apart from Christ received no mercy.

1 Peter 2:9–10 (KJV)

"But ye are a chosen generation, a royal priesthood, a holy nation, a peculiar people; that ye should shew forth

*the praises of him who hath called you out of darkness
into his marvelous light: Which in time past were not
a people but are now the people of God: which had not
obtained mercy, but now have obtained mercy."*

NUGGET THREE

My friends, Jesus' light eliminates the darkness! The very chaos of life. Think about it. God formed creation out of chaos when He said let there be light. If you are seeking a way out of darkness and chaos . . . seek Jesus! Jesus says:

John 12:46
*"I am come a light into the world, that whosoever
believeth on me should not abide in darkness"*

Again, do you yearn to know how the chaos you are going through will end? Will you survive it, or will it defeat you? Are you looking for direction through the chaos?

Then put your hand in the Savior's hand, my friends, for He has already defeated this world and its darkness! I leave you with one of my favorite Psalms:

Psalm 27:1–5 (KJV)
*[1]"The LORD is my light and my salvation; whom shall I
fear? the LORD is the strength of my life; of whom shall
I be afraid?
[2] When the wicked, even mine enemies and my foes, came
upon me to eat up my flesh, they stumbled and fell.
[3] Though a host should encamp against me, my heart*

shall not fear: though war should rise against me, in this will I be confident.
⁴ One thing have I desired of the LORD, that will I seek after; that I may dwell in the house of the LORD all the days of my life, to behold the beauty of the LORD, and to enquire in his temple.
⁵ For in the time of trouble he shall hide me in his pavilion: in the secret of his tabernacle shall he hide me; he shall set me up upon a rock."

My friends it is time to become Saints! Don't delay! As Adrian Rogers puts it:

"It is safer on the waves with Jesus than on the boat without Him!"

If you are ready to walk the waves with Jesus by learning more about surrendering to Him send me an email and I will help you. If you need prayer for direction for yourself or a loved one, send me an email, and I will pray with you.

Friends, tomorrow is not promised. As Joshua said, *"Choose you today who you will serve . . ."*

God Bless!

BE INSPIRED AS YOU WAIT AND TRUST
Psalm 33:18–22

Saints, have you ever been depressed, worried, dismayed or downright captured by circumstances that seem to drain your energy? Draining it to the point that your spirit is impacted? Some folks use to say that it seems like Satan himself is sitting on your back porch.

This portion of Psalms reminds us that whatever we are going through our Lord has his loving, compassionate, and caring eye on those who are His. How do I know that? Glad you asked! Because he said that His eye is upon those who *fear* Him!

NUGGET ONE

Saints, the psalmist is reminding us that even though our Lord can see all as He is omnipresent, He has a special eye on those who obey, serve, and glorify Him—Saints, who have given their lives to Him to care for and protect. Our Lord does not want His people to be tangled up in worry, depression, or being dismayed in any circumstances. To do so would imply we have a Father who ignores our needs! Instead this Psalm is clear in that our Lord has a SPECIAL eye on those who are His!

The psalmist further inspires God's people that God's eye is on those who "hope in His mercy." In other words, those believers who "wait and trust" in the Lord. It is so awesome how our Father's Word is never out of place. Look at how our Lord through this psalmist first said that we must "fear," meaning serve, obey, and glorify Him! Now he says to hope in His mercy.

NUGGET TWO

Saints, we need to serve, obey, and glorify our Father through our worry, depression, and situations that cause us to be dismayed. When we do this, our praise will help us be more than conquerors as we become inspired to wait and trust.

Romans 8:37
"Nay, in all these things we are more than conquerors through him that loved us."

Now, the psalmist is reminding us what to wait and trust for—deliverance from death and being kept alive in famine. In other words, that if we wait, we can be assured that our Lord will supply all our needs and comfort during these times. In making particular reference to famine, it was noted that in those days it was not surprising to witness God's people surviving famine while others did not.

NUGGET THREE

Saints, look at verse 20. I love how it starts with **"OUR,"** referring to those who have been inspired to wait and trust. Those who are more than conquerors. Those who have been inspired to wait as they continue to serve, obey, and glorify God through their particular trial. This soul now recognizes our Father as "our help and shield." Finding rest in the Lord as they wait and trust.

Saints, this is a confidence that can only come from a couple of sources. As were serve, obey, and glorify Him we take our eye off our situation and realize that His eye is upon us. Secondly, as we walk with Him more and more we will learn to lean on Him more and more and not on ourselves!

Psalm 3:5–6
"Trust in the Lord with all thine heart; and lean not unto thine own understanding. In all thy ways acknowledge him, and he shall direct thy paths."

Saints, are you at rest and peace trusting and waiting on the Lord? If not, get busy serving, obeying, and glorifying Him . . . *NOW!*

Verse 21, *"for our heart shall rejoice in Him, because we have trusted in His holy name!"* That word *trust* is now in the past tense meaning that we have finally experienced the awesome blessing of trusting in our Lord, thereby bringing as Paul says, *"a peace which passeth all understanding."* We rejoice because we have within us a Lord that is above all gods! A mighty God! A loving God! We as Saints have all that God is within us . . . Halleluiah!

HOLD ON! There is a requirement that we must recognize! Please allow me to preface this in the following manner. I often say as our choir or congregation sings that we are to be ever careful what we are singing. Gospel songs are so inspiring that we can get caught up in the beat and melody and lose sight of the words that offer commitment to the Savior, that if some would stop and think would sadly clear their throat when they got to that part of the song. Sadly, the same can be said here as we embrace verse 22.

NUGGET FOUR

Saints, the psalmist now closes with a great confidence in the mercy of our Father. He also has a remarkable confidence in waiting and trusting as he says that the Lord's mercy is to be given according as the Saint waits and trusts in the Lord. My friends, the more you wait and trust in the Lord and realize the blessings that wait for you, then waiting and trusting becomes a habit and a remedy for your worry, depression, and situations that may cause you to be dismayed. Because we know that our God will give us more than we can ever imagine!

Do you believe this? Have you been inspired to wait and trust in the Lord by serving, obeying, and glorifying Him throughout your trials? Has this become a habit in your Christian walk? Is it a remedy you have learned to lean on?

I leave you with this Scripture:

Ephesians 3:20–21

"Now unto him that is able to do exceeding abundantly above all that we ask or think, according to the power that worketh in us, Unto him be glory in the church by Christ Jesus throughout all ages, world without end. Amen."

God Bless!

BECOMING A FRIEND OF GOD
Genesis 18:10-15

Saints, each of us usually has more acquaintances than true friends. A friend that you can count on no matter what. A friend that we use to say always "got your back."

A friend who will cry with you. A friend who will listen to you without judging you. A friend who shares your sadness and your joy with the same love and compassion for you in both instances. A friend who can "tell you like it is" without hurting your feelings. A friend who understands. You get the point. An acquaintance is nice, but a friend is awesome!

The real question is, how does one become a friend of God? Many times, as God's children we pray to God as an acquaintance rather than a friend that we can count on. For example, when God promises that He will supply all our needs, one can pray and yet doubt whether this is in fact true.

To become a friend of God, we must first know God as OMNIPOTENT, meaning that God can bring to pass everything that He chooses, NO EXCEPTIONS!

Satan's world will try to break up this friendship by presenting circumstances that appear to be too big for our God. Those in these situations, if not careful, can find themselves praying to our God as an acquaintance rather than a friend. You know the prayer, "God please come to my aide by your riches and glory . . ." and before we get off our knees we doubt whether God will show up.

🥜 NUGGET ONE

Oh, ye of little faith. In our passage of Scripture, Sarah thought this and even laughed within herself when she heard that God had said that she would bear a son in her old age. My friends, there is nothing too big for our God! If God says it, then that settles it . . . period! God promised to take care of us and never, ever leave us. And that should settle it . . . period! We must go boldly before His throne never doubting but standing on our faith. Thus, pleasing God as we tell Him all about our troubles!

Hebrews 11:6
"But without faith it is impossible to please him: for he that cometh to God must believe that he is, and that he is a rewarder of them that diligently seek him."

However, the world will laugh and scoff at this faith we have in our God. Giving all glory to man, superheroes and such . . .

My favorite black-and-white movie of all time is *A Raisin in the Sun*—not the new ones as they do not demonstrate the passion that this one does. However, there is a scene where a young daughter says that she is going to be a doctor and her mother attempts to encourage her and says, "That is great, Lord willing."

I wanted to applaud when I heard her reply as the book of James reminds us that we should be ever carful of what we are going to do and plan without God. However, her daughter made me run for cover. Her reply to her mother's godly response was that God has nothing to do with it and that there is only man, and she was tired that God gets all the credit instead of man.

Now, today that would sell tickets but then all of us that had grandmothers that we use to call "Big Momma" knew what was coming next and it would not be pretty. But even today when I watch this scene, it brings tears to my eyes the strength of "Big Momma" and her trust and faith in God. Especially her very dramatic response! (Rent it, you will love it!)

NUGGET TWO

Saints, Sarah "laughed" at the omnipotence of God, ignoring also His omnipresence as well. It should be alarming for all of us when we fail to recognize that God sees our hearts as He listens to our words. He knows when they do not match. You can't clothe God's divine promises by your coat of disbelief and expect to receive or see the promise. Saints, we do this when we attempt to qualify God's divine promises with earthly standards. A friend of God believes and NEVER disbelieves in God's promises. Not just openly but inwardly as well. Unbelief is an insult to God and keeps us from being a friend of God. When one allows human standards to overtake them, they must confess and repent of this unbelief. Look at Job who humbled himself . . .

Job 42:1–2 (Amplified)
"Then Job said to the Lord, ² 'I know that You can do all things, and that no thought or purpose of Yours can be restrained or thwarted.'"

You want to be a friend of God? Let's look at another lady in **Luke 1:34–37**. Mary was told that she would have a child even though she "knew" no man! She never doubted or laughed but simply wanted to know how.

Our God's answer is very noteworthy for those today when tempted by Satan to doubt the strength, power, and omniscience of our God. Look at God's answer in verse 35. God says that the Holy Ghost shall come upon Mary! However, look at what follows "and." God says that "the power of the Highest shall overshadow thee."

NUGGET THREE

Saints, God is assuring Mary that He Himself will look after this matter and that He is in control. In other words, He is telling Mary as we would say, "I, your God, got this." Saints, this is how we should approach our God knowing that whatever we may be going through that our God "Got this"! That He will look after the matter. When you as His children of light embrace this, you become a friend of God. For as verse 37 declares, ***"For with God nothing shall be impossible."***

Do you believe this? Do you want to be a friend of God? Do you want to know His omniscience? Send me an email and I will communicate this Gospel to you that your joy may be filled . . .

I leave you with this Scripture:

Psalm 115:1–3

"Not unto us, O Lord, not unto us, but unto thy name give glory, for thy mercy, and for thy truth's sake.
² Wherefore should the heathen say, 'Where is now their God?' 3 But our God is in the heavens: he hath done whatsoever he hath pleased."

God Bless!

DAILY OUR GOD SAVES US FROM OURSELVES

Saints, remember Flip Wilson's portrayal of the character Geraldine? In all of Geraldine's mishaps, her answer when caught was, "The devil made me do it!" As a family in Chicago, we would sit in the living room watching *The Flip Wilson Show* and laugh about Geraldine and her trademark excuse about the "devil."

Today we still see this trademark excuse being given by those who mistakenly attribute more power to Satan than he has. Unwittingly, even those saints set apart by our God have said things like, "The devil got me today," or "The devil beat me up today."

Saints, we can give Satan too much power and certainly more credit than he deserves for our calamities!

NUGGET ONE

James 1:14–15 reminds us that we are tempted when we are drawn away by OUR OWN lusts! In other words, Satan can place something before us, but we are lured and attracted by our own lusts. Once we respond by this we have turned this enticement into sin. Saints, it is not Satan with the power, it is we who have choices!

That is why we need our Heavenly Father to save us daily from ourselves as Christians . . . Amen!

Psalm 32:1-4

How does God save us from ourselves? King David is a perfect example as he was a man after God's own heart **(Acts 13:22)**. In this portion of Psalms, we see David very remorseful about His sin of immorality and murder. He looks to God for forgiveness and saving him from himself.

He begins by recognizing the compassion and love He has for him as His child. He relies on God's compassion by saying first that blessed is the man whose transgressions are forgiven. *The Amplified Bible* puts it this way: "happy and to be envied is this man!" Why? Because forgiving our transgressions are "constantly" upon us as God's children. *Amplified* further says it is a blessing like the air we breathe!

David further says that God is so compassionate towards us that he "imputed not iniquity," meaning that he attributes no charges, crime, nor injustice for those who confess their sin to God!

NUGGET TWO

So, saints, should we let the "sin party" begin? Absolutely not!

Romans 6:1–2

"What shall we say then? Shall we continue in sin, that grace may abound? ² God forbid. How shall we, that are dead to sin, live any longer therein?"

Saints, our old self has been crucified with Christ that we no longer serve sin but walk in NEWNESS of life! David had been silent for his unconfessed sin for too long. The text says that his bones had *"waxed old"* and that he felt the hand of displeasure of the Lord day and night *"heavy upon him"*! A saint set apart by God does not have peace with unconfessed sin. These sins of David aged him, and God's displeasure was weighed upon him day and night to the point he could not even cry tears of relief anymore. David ends the verse with "Selah," meaning to ponder and think about it . . . been there, saints? To the world these sins would be "business as usual" without any remorse, but not to a child of the Most High!

So, what is the first step of our God to daily save us from ourselves? Good question! Glad you asked! We must go to **Psalm 51:1–3** for the first step!

David was convicted and acknowledged that in his transgressions he had stepped outside the moral boundaries established by God. He also was convicted and acknowledges his iniquities were wrong and without excuse. That is the textual meaning of both. Further, he had missed the mark set by God with his sin.

NUGGET THREE

Saints, David was at a point where he was so low that he had no other way to look but up. We know that our Bible gives us the moral and physical boundaries that we are to follow as we walk in the ways of our Lord. When we "miss the mark," this should trouble our spirits to the point of misery knowing that our Father is not pleased! One place of reckoning is the strain it puts on our prayer life as we pray with unconfessed sin in our life. Praying for "this and that" and "for others" all the while hearing the Holy Spirit whispering in our ears the question, "When are you going to pray for you and your unconfessed sin?" Saints, unconfessed sin will and does hinder our prayer life!

So, the first step in allowing God to daily save us from ourselves is to **"to be convicted of our sin and acknowledge it"**!

David's first step of \acknowledging and being convicted of his sin drove him to pray for pardon. At the point where Nathan told him of his sin, David could have had Nathan killed and continued in his sin and no one would be any wiser . . . except for God! My friends, without acknowledging and being convicted of our sin, we will never turn to God for pardon and will miss out on the compassion He has for us to save us from ourselves. I leave you with David's acknowledgement:

Psalm 51:2–3
"Wash me thoroughly from mine iniquity, and cleanse me from my sin. ³ For I acknowledge my transgressions: and my sin is ever before me."

God Bless!

CARING FOR THE EYE OF GOD

In the last nugget we explored Part 1 of the topic *"Our God Saves Us From Ourselves."* In looking at David's prayer of confession, **Psalm 51**, we realized that the first step in allowing our God to save us from ourselves is to acknowledge and be convicted of our sin.

Now we will look at Part 2, the need for us to "care for the eye of God." **Job 34:21–22** reminds us of the following:

"For his eyes are upon the ways of man, and he seeth all his goings. There is no darkness, nor shadow of death, where the workers of iniquity may hide themselves."

NUGGET ONE

Saints, this reminds us that the eye of God is on all that we do! That we cannot hide anything from Him! We may be able to hide our sin from each other, our pastor, parents, or friends, but we can NEVER hide them from our God! Someone wrote "it is like a thief stealing in the very sight of the judge." As a saint set apart by God, we care for the eye of God because we realize that he is witnessing our sins as we do them and they grieve Him.

That is why David is first taking his sin to the throne of God in Psalm 51. First, acknowledging and being convicted of his sin. However, next he realized what he had in verse 4, ". . . done this evil in thy (God's) sight . . ."

Saints, for our God to save us from ourselves we must cherish the eye of God and do all we can not to grieve Him by sinning. Any wonder why David said in this same verse that His sin was against God and God ONLY!

NUGGET TWO

Saints, David had surely sinned against both Uriah and Bathsheba, breaking up their marriage. He also sinned against their families by murder, yet why would he say against God only? The best answer is given by Charles Haddon Spurgeon who writes, ***"The virus of sin lies in its opposition to God: The psalmist sense of sin towards others rather tended to increase the force of his feeling of sin against God. All wrongdoing centered, culminated, and came to a climax, at the foot of the divine throne."***

Saints, when we realize and care for the eye of God, we take our sin first to the throne of God, not man. It is God who grieves, and His grief should motivate us to repent! Turning from our sin to God! Sure, David was remorseful for what he had done to Uriah and Bathsheba, but he had done a lot more to God. God who had brought him a mighty long way. He had brought him from a shepherd boy to a king. Saints, how far has our God brought YOU? Do you have unrepentant sin that is grieving Him? Have you asked for forgiveness from those you have wronged but have never gone to God to ask His forgiveness, indicating that you care for the eye of God? As Spurgeon says, "All wrongdoing centered, culminated, and came to a climax, at the foot of the divine throne." Go there, Saints!

Then one of the most awesome verses is verse 6 where David acknowledges that our God sees our inner being as well as he sees our outer being. That our God *"desirest truth in the inward parts . . ."* My friends, you may as well be truthful with our God because he already knows!

I am reminded of something my parents us to say to me and I also said to my children. We all should be familiar with this as we would say to them, "Tell me the truth and your punishment will not be as bad!" Remember? I tried a few times to sway the truth in my favor but would always get caught. It wasn't until I was a parent that I realized that as a parent, I knew the truth and waited to see if my children would own up to it. That's why I got caught because my parents knew the truth before they asked me.

My friend, God knows the truth from your inner parts before you confess! David recognized that he was *"shapen in iniquity."* Not that his parents brought him into the world sinfully but that he had a sinful nature.

NUGGET THREE

Saints, we all have a sinful nature. Look at David. One day he was in good standing with God and the next he was an adulterer and a murderer! Saints, we all can and have fallen from grace for we too have been *"shapen in iniquity"* by Adam's original sin. That is the very reason we are to "care for the eye of God as we walk this Christian journey. **Psalm 91** reminds us to *"abide under the shadow of the almighty."*

My friends, if we live our lives under the shadow of our God, we will learn to care for His eye upon us and realize that He is our secret place of refuge. Amen!

Then finally, as we end part 2 of our God daily saving us from ourselves, look at David saying, *". . . thou shalt make me to know wisdom."*

🏷 FINAL NUGGET

Saints, when David says this he is recognizing that as he is truthful, acknowledging his sin and recognizing that he had done all this in the eye of God and confessed it at His throne, God had given him wisdom! My friends, that wisdom was that no matter how good David thought he was or how wretched he could be, God revealed to him that he has a sin nature that is worse than David could ever imagine. You say, how is that wisdom?

Saints, when we look in the mirror after God has shown us how wretched we truly are, we began to reverence Him for His knowledge and desire to save us from ourselves. For we now have come into the realization that we cannot save ourselves, much less save us from ourselves because we are wretched beyond belief even in our own minds. You ever do something wrong that surprised even you? If not, my mom and grandmother use to say, "Live long enough and you will!" This is the wisdom that David is referring to. Saints, this is the wisdom that should keep us at the foot of our Father's throne seeking to daily be saved from ourselves.

Proverbs 1:7
"The fear of the Lord is the beginning of knowledge: but fools despise wisdom and instruction."

God Bless!

EARTH'S UNIVERSAL SONG

Psalm 66:1–4 (KJV)
*"Make a joyful noise unto God, all ye lands:
Sing forth the honour of his name: make his praise
glorious. Say unto God, How terrible art thou in thy
works! through the greatness of thy power shall thine
enemies submit themselves unto thee. All the earth shall
worship thee and shall sing unto thee; they shall sing to
thy name. Selah."*

Saints, while today we have our congregational praises limited to churches and worship events, David is speaking of a day when all God's lands will recognize who he is and praise Him from every land. Different continents, languages, cultures, times, ages, male and female, kings and servants, free and imprisoned, ALL will sing praises to our God in a universal song from Earth! WOW, just imagine!

🪨 NUGGET ONE

Saints, imagine David sent this psalm to his best musician to put to music. Can you imagine how the music must have sounded with such awesome words of hope and praise? Imagine today if this music with these words were to be played on every radio station around the world!

David is not just saying to make a noise but a JOYFUL noise! My friends, that type of noise can only come from a heart that has been delivered. Delivered from the very threshold of hell! Delivered from justifiable condemnation to a loving unity with a most gracious and merciful God, honoring His name only!

Imagine, Saints, no more songs about prosperity, degrading our women, war, violence, pride and degradation! Only one unified song and voice honoring only our Creator, Sustainer, Deliverer, Only Father . . . God! No songs to Buddha, Saints, Mary, Angels BUT ONLY to God! An unimpeded praise to only Him that is worthy of our praise! "All the earth" honoring His name alone, making His praise glorious! Doesn't this bring a humbling chill and goosebumps to a heart sold out for our God?

NUGGET TWO

Saints, a quote from The Treasury of David says:

*"Power brings a man to his knee,
but love alone wins his heart."*

Saints, when we see the power of our God to deliver wretches like we were, one can only drop to our knee in reverence to an awesome God. But that power oozing with love wins more than our souls but our hearts as well. That is why we cannot help but praise Him! We cannot help but trust and rely on Him. That is why our hearts praise Him as "MY God"!

We long for that day as David says in **Psalm 22:27**

"All the ends of the world shall remember and turn unto the LORD: and all the kindreds of the nations shall worship before thee."

Amen?

God Bless!

NUGGETS TO LIVE BY

fAITH HONORS GOD AND GOD HONORS fAITH

Saints, there was this old lady who worked in a hotel frequented by traveling salesmen as they came to town on business. All looked forward to seeing her because of her peaceful spirit.

It was awesome to witness this old lady singing and praising God throughout the day! As she would clean the rooms, she would sing songs such as "Amazing Grace," "How Great Thou Art," "Blessed Assurance," and more! Never complaining and always happy in such a way that it was contagious to anyone in her presence. Many said she reminded them of their mothers and it was like being at home away from home.

Then a new traveling saleswoman was in the hotel and noticed the old lady and was very perplexed as to how someone could be so happy in such a job. She went to the old lady and said, "It seems very obvious that you love God." To which the old lady replied, "I certainly love my God because He first loved me!"

The saleswoman said, "But what if you lost your job? What would you do?" The old lady said, "I'll talk to my God!" The saleswoman again asked, "But what would you do if you became injured and could not work?" The old lady again said, "I'll talk to my God!" The saleswoman, frustrated, began to ask, "But what if . . ." when she was interrupted by the old woman.

The old woman looked at the saleswoman and said, "You live too much in the "ifs" of life. I live in the "whatever" in life!" Then she further said, "I live knowing that my God will supply *whatever* I need because I trust Him!"

NUGGET ONE

Saints, a country preacher by the name of Adrian Rogers put it this way, "What we need is not great faith but faith in a great God." As we walk this Christian journey, our Father honors such faith in Him, whereby we trust Him with everything.

Anything less dishonors God and such weak faith can put us in position to doubt the greatness of our Father and His love towards us. Imagine if the old lady had given the traveling saleswoman an answer implying that any hardship would cause her to break and be defeated. The ministry that drew many to her would have been weakened and possibly been destroyed by one wrong answer.

Romans 8:35–37 (KJV)

"Who shall separate us from the love of Christ? shall tribulation, or distress, or persecution, or famine, or nakedness, or peril, or sword? As it is written, For thy sake we are killed all the day long; we are accounted as sheep for the slaughter. Nay, in all these things we are more than conquerors through him that loved us."

NUGGET TWO

Saints, sometimes we all go through a rough spell where our faith may appear to weaken. It is specifically in those times that our faith should instead be strengthened by the rigors of the trial we may be experiencing!

God's Word says we are MORE THAN CONQUERORS, meaning that we have more than we need within us to conquer anything that may come upon us. More to spare! That is Christ in us! Yes, we may bend but we will not break! That is why we praise God through the storms of life as they draw us closer to Him.

Saints, our Father will take whatever we are going through and make it for our good no matter what it is:

Romans 8:28 (KJV)
"And we know that all things work together for good to them that love God, to them who are the called according to his purpose."

So, praise Him, saints, through it all and just like the old lady said about pending trials, "I'll talk to my Father!"

Do you think she knew this promise from God? Do you?

1 Corinthians 10:13 (KJV)
"There hath no temptation taken you but such as is common to man: but God is faithful, who will not suffer you to be tempted above that ye are able; but will with the temptation also make a way to escape, that ye may be able to bear it."

God Bless!

NUGGETS TO LIVE BY

GLORY BE TO THE NAME OF THE LORD!
Psalm 107

Saints, what an awesome Psalm that reminds us of how and why the name of our Lord should be glorified!

Have you been seeking the Lord continuously? Have you taken the time throughout the year to ponder on the rich goodness, mercy, and grace of our Lord? Have you given Him glory by exalting Him and Him alone this year?

NUGGET ONE

Saints, four times in this Psalm (verses 8, 15, 21 and 31) the writer pleads:

"Oh that men would praise the Lord for His goodness, and for His wonderful works to the children of men!"

Each stanza is a remembrance of how our Lord has revealed Himself and delivered us from some type of catastrophic dilemma. Been there, Saints? Saints, our minds many times suffer from "selective recall." By that I mean we soon forget those times when our Lord snatched us from the jaws of defeat. When our Lord snatched us from the utter darkness of this sinful world. Saved us from wondering in the darkness . . . lost!

Saints, remember when we cried out in those moments past for our Lord to deliver us? When we cried out realizing there was nowhere else to go? We had sunk so low there was nowhere else to look but up! Halleluiah, we saw our Lord on the throne waiting for us to seek His face! A loving face that was all too ready and prepared to deliver us from our current dilemma:

> *"Oh that men would praise the Lord for His goodness,*
> *and for His wonderful works to the children of men!"*

NUGGET TWO

Saints, in this Psalm we also see that those who found themselves in trouble sought our Lord each time (verses 6, 13, 19 and 28):

> *"Then they cried unto the Lord in their trouble . . ."*

Saints, we serve a great deliverer! Seek his face in times of trouble! Seek His face continuously! Notice that in this Psalm there was not a prayer for help before they sought help elsewhere. As saints we must continuously reside at the throne of our Lord! They only cried out *"in their trouble."* Saints, we must not be in the habit of only crying out to our Lord when we are down and troubled. Instead we must continually praise Him for His goodness and mercy towards us, His children . . . Amen?

Saints, let's not make a habit of limited praise but a continuous praise! For some of you this may be a beginning so never let the praise end or become limited!

Isaiah 26:3
"Thou wilt keep him in perfect peace,
whose mind is stayed on thee: because he trusteth
in thee."

Saints, this Psalm also reminds us that when God delivers us He delivers us completely! God does not "put a bandage on our dilemma." His deliverance is complete. After all, God alone knows what we need now and into eternity.

Psalm 107:35–37
"He turneth the wilderness into a standing water, and
dry ground into waterspings. And there he maketh
the hungry to dwell, that they may prepare a city for
habitation; And sow the fields, and plant vineyards,
which may yield fruits of increase."

Saints, what an awesome God we have the privilege of serving! We must serve and praise Him continually! During this season many will seek His face and, praise God, will find Him! Just remember our Lord is too precious to place on a shelf and bring Him out in times of trouble or just for a season! Let all that seek Him commit to make Him a "way of life" as we walk this Christian journey through the wilderness of this world!

Psalm 107:43

"Whoso is wise, and will observe these things, even they shall understand the loving kindness of the LORD."

Friends, if you are ready to learn more about surrendering to our Lord, send me an email and I will help you. If you need prayer for direction for yourself or a love one send me an email and I will pray with you.

Friends, tomorrow is not promised. As Joshua said, *"Choose you today who you will serve . . ."*

God Bless!

GOD DOES NOT COMFORT US TO BE COMFORTABLE

Saints, our God will deliver, heal, provide, protect, comfort, and abundantly much more! However, our God does not comfort us to be comfortable. One of the most read chapters of comfort is John 14:

John 14:1 (KJV)
¹ "Let not your heart be troubled: ye believe in God, believe also in me."

Saints, God comforts us to be a comfort to others. In this chapter Jesus was on the way to the cross and took this opportunity to comfort His disciples in preparation for the ministry work required of them after His resurrection.

Saints, we too have ministry work to do! God has blessed us with the comfort of His Most Holy Word and His promises that will never fail. Ah, but He did not do this for us to sit in our spiritual Lazy-Boy chairs or just to sit in the church pew! We must realize that our responsibility is to be "COMFORTERS"!

🄽 NUGGET ONE

Saints, look with me to **Isaiah 40:1–2**:

¹ "Comfort ye, comfort ye my people, saith your God. ² Speak ye comfortably to Jerusalem, and cry unto her, that her warfare is accomplished, that her iniquity is pardoned: for she hath received of the LORD'S hand double for all her sins."

Isaiah was comforted by God that God had heard the cry of the people. That a remnant of them were pardon for their egregious sins and that they had paid double for them. Can you imagine the comfort Isaiah must have felt to know that God had mercy upon the people and offered His forgiveness to them?

God told Isaiah to *"comfort ye my people."* Isaiah had no time to sit in the blessing of God's comfort. God immediately told him to comfort His people.

Saints, we have all been comforted with the grace of God's pardon for our egregious sins as well! Are we now to sit back in the church pews and bask in our deliverance comfortably or get up and go comfort others with the great news of God's Gospel that is able to comfort those who are lost?

🄽 NUGGET TWO

The people had paid double for their sins, but Christ paid the price for ours! Saints, we must be COMFORTERS for others and tell the lost about "our" awesome loving God who desires that all men be saved. As Isaiah was told to tell them *"saith **your** God"*!

This denotes a relationship between believers and God. A relationship that is unbreakable, loving, merciful, and unlike any other. A relationship built on the blood of the One who paid the price, our Savior, Jesus Christ! Furthermore, we are to speak this Gospel "comfortably" with others.

Saints, the lost should hear and feel the message of comfort that so comforts us. This message of comfort should come from your heart to their heart. Saints, that's your testimony of what your God has done to comfort you. Have you recently shared from your heart your testimony with those who are lost? If so, praise God! If not, why not?

Saints, I was giving a Bible study in a nursing home recently and an elderly woman said she believed in Jehovah but that she was not certain of her salvation, but she did not believe in hell or Christ! This lady was prepared to die and be in her grave without the hope of Heaven! I could not leave her side without sharing the certainty of Heaven that she could have in Jesus Christ! Could you?

How many times has God caused the lost in your families, neighborhoods, and jobs cross your path while you have remained silent? Remaining silent while embracing the comfort of your deliverance and hope of Heaven without sharing, Saints?

Saints, there was a prophet named Jeremiah who tried to hold God's Word in his heart without sharing. Look what happened to him:

Jeremiah 20:9 (AMP)
⁹ "If I say, I will not make mention of [the Lord] or speak any more in His name, in my mind and heart it is as if there were a burning fire shut up in my bones. And I am weary of enduring and holding it in; I cannot [contain it any longer]."

Is this you? Why not if you have been comforted and indwelt with the Holy Spirit of God? For we are all without excuse to share the good news of the Gospel!

God Bless!

2

GOD IS!

NUGGETS TO LIVE BY

GOD IS!

Saints, God's Word reminds us that we should know that **"God is"**!

Hebrews 11:6 (KJV)
⁶"But without faith it is impossible to please him: for he that cometh to God must believe that he is, and that he is a rewarder of them that diligently seek him."

Saints, when we know that **"God is,"** that is a combination of all He represents to us, His children. The song writer writes, *"**God is** my light in darkness, **God is** my joy in the time of sorrow, **God is** the joy and strength of my life, **God is** my all and all, and God will never fall short of His Word."* The song writer finishes by saying because ***God is,*** the song writer will never turn back.

Oh Saints, do you know God as **"God is"**? Have you walked with God long enough in sincerity to realize that He is so much to you that words could not explain it sufficiently? He has done so much that all you can do is simply say ***"God is"***?

There is a woman in 2 Kings 4:1–7 who had lost her husband and was left with two sons and much debt and nothing to pay that debt. The creditors were after her two sons to become bondsmen (indenture servants) to pay off the debt.

However, faced with this dilemma this woman knew **"God is"**! There are four Nuggets to help us today determine if we in fact know as this woman did that **"God is"**!

🥮 NUGGET ONE

Saints, nowhere is it said that this woman complained or was fearful. Let us look at what she did first. She **TRUSTED GOD** by going to the prophet Elisha. She came to him expressing that her husband reverenced God and one must realize that he taught his family to do the same. Ah Saints, she was approaching God how He wants to be approached in faith, trusting Him! The Psalmist says:

Psalm 37:25 (KJV)
[25] "I have been young, and now am old; yet have I not seen the righteous forsaken, nor his seed begging bread."

Today, Saints, because of the blood of Jesus Christ we can go directly to God. When you go to God are you covered by the blood? When you go to God are you doubting His power and desire to deliver you? When you go to God and pray and before you get up from your knees, are you seeking your own plan versus the plan God has for you? The question, Saints, is then, *Do you really know "God is"*?

🥮 NUGGET TWO

This woman demonstrated her faith and trust in God by **LISTENING FOR GOD'S PLAN!** Yes! Saints, when this woman presented her situation to Elisha she waited to hear God's plan.

There was no doubt clouding her eyes, ears, and heart to God's plan because she knew that **"God is."**

Saints, how often do you pray lacking patience thinking that God is not listening? Allowing doubt to cloud your eyes, ears, and heart to the plan God has just for you for your particular situation? Again, do you know that **"God is"**?

NUGGET THREE

The third lesson is that after this woman heard the plan, she was **OBEDIENT**! She was given instructions that seemed impossible and humiliating. She was told to go to her neighbors and get all their empty vessels and bring them to her house and get behind closed doors and pour her pot of oil in them until they were all full.

Wow! This woman followed God's plan without doubt or whining! Saints, how many of you would look at God's plan and doubt it because you cannot understand it in your finite minds, ignoring that **"God is"**? Imagine this woman pouring from her pot into many larger vessels and yet the oil kept coming! How many times has God told you that He will give you an increase if you just obey?

When she followed God's plan, He poured out blessings that were overflowing. Ah, Saints, imagine the praising that her and her sons were doing as they witnessed God's miracle alone with each other! Feeling the very presence of God! Realizing the confirmation that **"God is"** together!

Imagine, Saints, as Mom was pouring, she asked her sons to bring another empty vessel to which they replied there were no empty ones left. God had filled them all from their small pot! The Scripture says the oil ceased. Saints, God gave them exactly what they needed to the last drop!

Saints, how many times has God given you exactly what you needed? What did you do with it? Did you go back to God or did you squander it? This woman did something that we all must learn from as we continue our walk with our Lord.

NUGGET FOUR

The final point is that this woman did not take the blessing that God gave her and proceed with her plan. How many times when you receive your blessing do you take the opportunity to carry out your plan instead of God's plan? Verse 7 reminds us, Saints, that when we are blessed we are to **GO BACK TO GOD AND SEEK HIS DIRECTION AS TO WHAT TO DO WITH IT!** Making sure we carry out His plan for us and not ours!

2 Kings 4:6–7 (KJV)
7 "Then she came and told the man of God. And he said, 'Go, sell the oil, and pay thy debt, and live thou and thy children of the rest.'"

Saints, do you really know God as "GOD IS"?

God Bless!

GOD'S PROMISES CAN BUCKLE YOUR KNEES

Saints, when we embrace the fact that God's promises rest on four things, we cannot help but to rely on His promises. We know that man's promises many times are truly worthless and many times are subject to conditions.

However, our God's promises are based on our God's justice and holiness in that He cannot and will not deceive us! Also, our God's awesome grace and goodness in that He will not forget His promises to us.

Man will sometimes change his promises based on conditions; however, our God's truth assures us as His children that He will not change. Finally, our God can do exactly what He promises He will do!

In **1 Chronicles 17:16** David knew that God's promises were based on all these factors and more. David had longed to build a temple for God, but God had other plans for David. Plans that buckled David's knees!

NUGGET ONE

Saints, have you ever sat and just pondered the promises that our Father has made to you? Promises of eternal life with Him.

Promises of deliverance from your trials or just the fact of knowing that He has promised to be with you in those trials guiding and protecting you.

Scripture says that after giving birth, Mary lay there and ponder on what had just happened. She had experienced a promise realized in God allowing her to deliver our Messiah into the world! Saints, have you sat and pondered on the promises you have realized each day? Promises that were just for you from God?

First Chronicles says that David sat before the Lord. David had just been told that the Messiah would come through his lineage. I envision David's knees buckled from the news that caused him to sit before the Lord in prayer. The custom was to kneel or lay prostrate, but David sat down!

Saints, if God has not caused your knees to buckle when you experience His promises just keep living for Him . . . you will!

David had received more than he expected! Saints, to your amazement, how many times has our Father given you more than you expected . . .?

NUGGET TWO

David sat there in amazement and said, *"Who am I?"* and ***"Thou has regarded me according to the estate of a man of high degree."*** David realized that God's promise was unmerited grace that humbled him and buckled his knees.

Saints, a very good friend of mine, always respond when asked by anyone how he is doing, "Blessed beyond what I deserve!" My friends, God knows us better than we know ourselves; hence, He knows what we need and is willing and able to do it for those who are His. Saints, have you realized His promises today and every day?

NUGGET THREE

Not only did David's knees buckle but he was speechless! David went on to say to our Father, *"What can I speak more to thee for the honor of thy servant . . ."* Oh, Saints, when our Father overwhelms us with His promises, we have to turn the TV off! Turn the computer off! Pull over to the side of the road! Hang up the phone! And anything else to be alone and ponder on His promises of unmerited grace! Ponder on the fact of what an awesome God we have the privilege of serving and praising! Saints, have you surrendered to Him today and put Him first today? Many of you probably did not yesterday!

Look at David's praise and worship after God buckled his knees and rendered him speechless. All David could say was:

1 Chronicles 17:20 (KJV)
[20] "O LORD, there is none like thee, neither is there any God beside thee . . ."

Praise Him alone, Saints!

God Bless!

NUGGETS TO LIVE BY

GOD ONLY IS OUR PRESENT HELP AND OUR ETERNAL HOPE
Psalm 146

Saints, we have just finished a very trying and wearisome time in our lives. No matter what side you are on with the elections, it has brought some of the worst out of us as a people, and in many cases even as Christians. One side claiming to have answers for mankind and another claiming the very same thing!

Each time these elections take place, neighbors are pitted against one another, families are divided. Churches are also feeling the same strife in its congregations. Yard signs of political affiliation are causing neighbors to see each other in a new light. Passing judgments and accusations between each other and in many cases not verbal but by their countenances as they drive or pass by one another.

Accusations are being spewed about by both sides of the political aisle to the point that even Christians ought to be ashamed of our society and what it has come to in perpetuating a political process that is detrimental to our own souls that have been called by our God to love one another as Christ has loved us!

Saints, we as children of the Most High need to look to David in this Psalm of praise. David reminds us that no matter what, he will praise God. That while he lives he will praise the King of Kings. David's implication is that he knew he would not live forever but praises, while here, would continually come from his being. Every hour would be given in praise to God!

David knew that his life was a gift of mercy from God, and God deserved to be glorified, exalted, and praised by that life! That is why he said he "will sing praises unto my God while I have __any__ being"!

NUGGET ONE

Saints, no matter what outcome you wanted in the recent election, our focus while here on Earth is to be in glorifying, exalting, and praising our Heavenly Father no matter the situation. Our very lives are a gift of mercy from Him. We are to sing praises for as Christians we are to be happy in our present help and our hope for the future. This no man can give nor match what our Father desires for His children, no matter what political affiliation or political office. From Governor, State or U.S. Senator, or Congressman or Congresswoman!

The Psalm reminds us that our God *"made heaven and earth, the sea, and all that therein is."* He will execute judgment for the oppressed and loose the prisoners!

NUGGET TWO

Saints, David reminds us that we are not to put our trust in princes of which even he was one. We are not to rely on the great ones on Earth when we have The Great One in Heaven on His Throne! David reminds us of the great ones on Earth that *"his breath goeth forth, he returneth to his earth!"* In other words, counting on man is futile and ridiculous because when this man is without breath, he dies and his spirit goes one way (back to the Father) and his body another, back to the earth from which it was formed. My friends, man no matter how great we believe him to be, man is finite!

However, our God is infinite! When any great man has been separated from his spirit all his thoughts, promises, and all go with him. David says, *"In that very day his thoughts perish!"* Promises and all perish with him! We are to never put our hope as true Christians in man no matter how great he is nor the office he either holds or chooses to hold/!

Saints, only the promises of God will remain, for He alone is infinite and deserving of our praise and glory! Knowing this should cause us not to allow any politician or political party to stir strife and or hatred amongst us as Christians. Or at the very least to assume that man can do anything apart from Christ our Lord who told us that "a new commandment I leave for you, that you love one another as I have loved you and gave my life for you"! Saints, do you trust Him or man?

NUGGET THREE

Saints, the Lord NEVER dies nor does His thoughts! The Lord's desires for His children are alive even after "great men" perish! Any wonder why David says in **verse 5**:

> *"Happy is he that hath the God of Jacob for his help, whose hope is in the Lord his God!"*

Saints, to know God as the God of Jacob we must first know Him personally as our God. When this is a reality for the true believer, he can have a *"peace that passeth all understanding"* no matter what is going on around him! No matter who won or what political office is in charge. A true believer that has confidence in God will also have a happiness that cannot be explained to natural man.

This believer has walked with God over the years to the point that his confidence is based on the loving and merciful experience that he has received from his God! David says in **verse 8**:

> *"The Lord openeth the eyes of the blind: the Lord raiseth them that are bowed down: the Lord loveth the righteous . . ."*

Saints, we must trust in the Lord alone for *God only is our present help & our eternal hope!*

Any reason the Psalm starts this way:

> *"Praise ye the Lord. Praise the Lord, O my soul. ² While I live will I praise the Lord: I will sing praises unto my God while I have any being. ³ Put not your trust in princes, nor in the son of man, in whom there is no help."*

God Bless!

GOD, OUR WONDERFUL DELIVERER!
Colossians 1:12-14

What an awesome passage of Scripture for saints to meditate upon and ponder! To praise our Heavenly Father for His awesome love towards us who were once lost in the darkness of sin! When we read this Scripture, we realize that our Heavenly Father is in the business of populating the kingdom with souls for His Dear Son, Jesus Christ!

However, His sources for souls are captives in the power of darkness. Therefore, verse 12 says, *". . . made us meet to be partakers of the inheritance of the saints of light."* God had to make us "meet" or "FIT" to be partakers! Because before He delivered us, we were not qualified to enter the Kingdom. Romans 8:7 states that there was nothing in us but *"enmity to God."* Ephesians 2:1–8 further says that we *"walked according to the course of this world"* and walked with the demon spirit of disobedience . . . lost!

Held captive by the "POWER" of darkness! That power enslaved us before being delivered to stand in opposition to God.

That same power enslaves unbelievers today making them to be in opposition to God. Walking in the power of darkness, powerless in seeing their way out. With no help from others enslaved by this same power of darkness because no one has light within themselves to see their way out, blinded by the god of this world, Satan!

2 Corinthians 4:4
"In whom the god of this world hath blinded the minds of them which believe not, lest the light of the glorious gospel of Christ, who is the image of God, should shine unto them."

Only our wonderful Deliverer, God, could deliver us from the power of the god of this world. Our text uses the word *delivered* or *Erusato,* meaning *"to rescue"* or *"to snatch."*

NUGGET ONE
Saints, when we realize that only God could have rescued us out of the power of darkness by snatching us out, how could we ever desire to go back? He rescued us to be "partakers" of the inheritance with the saints in light! Meaning that once we believed and were set apart in the light of God, we too are saints! Saints made fit by God. Saints committed to living a life walking in the light of God. Yes, believers, we are saints made fit by God himself through the blood of His Dear Son, Jesus Christ, not man! Let us walk in His light always.

The text further says that as Saints, God has, *". . . translated us into the kingdom of His dear Son."*

NUGGET TWO

Saints, that Kingdom exists even today—in the spiritual realm with Jesus sitting at the right hand of the Father interceding on our behalf! Also, here on Earth within the hearts of His saints, you and me. Why would we ever want to go back to the power of darkness? **2 Peter 2:22** puts it this way, "... But it is happened unto them according to the true proverb (Prov. 26:11), 'The dog is turned to his own vomit again; and the sow that was washed to her wallowing in the mire.'"

Praise God for His Mercy and His Love for rescuing and snatching a wretch like us, Saints!

Unfortunately, we see professed Christians reverting back to the same vomit of darkness and even using God and His liberty erroneously as an excuse. I am reminded of the purpose our Savior came to this earth. Scripture is very clear in that he came to save the lost. Even the blind man in John that Jesus healed was shunned and kicked out of the temple after telling the Pharisees that all he knows is that, *"I was blind and now I see!"* Jesus sought him after the Pharisees turned their backs on him. Jesus asked him if he believed that he was the Son of God. The man who could see now said *"I believe"*!

NUGGET THREE

We to are called to seek the lost, Jude 22 and 23, "And of some have compassion, making a difference: And others save with fear, pulling them out of the fire; hating even the garment spotted by the flesh." We are to hate the sin but not the sinner! We have been given a Great Commission (Matt. 28:19–20)! Saints that walk in the light of Jesus are to reflect that light into the darkness to win souls for the Kingdom!

Second Corinthians 6:14 says that we should not be unequally yoked together with unbelievers. This is referring to any Spiritual enterprise or Spiritual relationship! This does not mean that we should end all associations with unbelievers! That would deny the reason God delivered (rescued/snatched) us out of darkness!

Saints, if you understand that God is our Wonderful Deliverer, all Glory belongs to Him. What better way to glorify our Heavenly Father than reflecting His light into this dark world of Satan, winning souls for the Kingdom of His Dear Son! For all we know, God will use someone who is a practicing homosexual who will see God's light reflected by us into this darkness to save that practicing homosexual and others that are enslaved by sin!

I leave you with this Scripture:

1 Corinthians 9:19
"For though I be free from all men, yet have I made myself servant unto all, that I might gain the more."

God Bless!

GOD SAYS, "HOLD MY HAND AND WALK WITH ME"
Psalm 73

Oh, what do we do when the world seems so unfair? When one feels that the world is on top of him instead of him on top of the world? What must one do when the pain of injustice and unfairness is visited upon him and his situation? Does one question God's sovereign power and question whether God even cares?

A musician by the name of Asaph experienced this pain and wrote a song that we read in Psalm 73. Psalms 50 and 73 through 83 are known as the "Psalms of Asaph," the director of music for David. In Psalm 73, Asaph was in pain as he continued to witness the unjust suffering of the poor believers while the wicked rich were prospering without suffering. To the point that he began to question why a just God would allow this unfairness . . . have you been there today?

However, there are lessons that he realized that are significant even today. Because one can make the case that the godly poor are experiencing the same even today. Let's look at the lesson that God gave to Asaph that is applicable to us today as God's children.

🟫 NUGGET ONE

Saints, we must continue to praise God through our pain! Asaph, in his pain, went to the Lord in the synagogue to praise and worship Him anyhow and it was there that he realized God's presence. *(Today as believers we do not have to go into a synagogue but through the blood of Jesus he dwells within the believer and all we must do is go to our knees!)

Asaph said it was not *until* he had talked with God through worship and praise that he now understood the end for the wicked and that God was holding his right hand leading him if he held on and followed. Can you imagine God holding our right hand as he leads us all the way to heaven as we kick up the gold dust on the streets, if only we keep our hand in His hand? **Hebrews 10:23** today reminds us to *"Let us hold fast to the profession of our faith, without wavering: (for he is faithful that promised)."*

🟫 NUGGET TWO

Secondly, Saints, we must remain focused on our Father's counseling through His Word, not man's! Once Asaph changed focus and started worshipping and praising God, he realized that God would provide divine guidance through *His* counsel! Who reading this must realize the necessity of divine counseling and guidance that only comes from the Lord, NOT man? Only through God's divine counseling and guidance can one be guided through the perils of wickedness and unfairness we see systematically being placed on the godly poor of today. One can only imagine and meditate on this and see God saying, *"Take my hand and hold on as you walk with me and I will see you through. Do not give a thought for the wicked and ungodly those that prosper today because their time is coming! Use the very breath of life I breathed into you to praise me not worry about the wicked!"*

God is saying allow me to divinely guide you as he said in **Philippians 1:6** where Paul came to this realization and said, *"Being confident of this very thing, that He which hath begun a good work in you will perform it until the day of Jesus Christ."*

During our adolescence we needed a level of guidance with limited trials. Why, at an older age, one believes that he requires less divine guidance to face more trials? One obviously needs more divine guidance not less . . . Amen?

NUGGET THREE

Third, we must realize that the promises of our God to us are eternal! Finally, Asaph realized this, praise God! That after all this injustice and unfairness by the wicked, prospering ungodly there will be glory, praise, and testimony realized in heaven for all those saints who hold on to the Lord's unchanging hand and follow Him alone! This prompted Asaph to write in **verse 25**, *"Whom have I in heaven but thee? And there is none upon earth that I desire beside thee!"*

John Calvin writes that "God will turn our wrong beginnings into happy endings." We must realize that God can, and we cannot! Our present is not our future. The ungodly rich bank on the present, but we know the future.

2 Corinthians 4:17–18 (KJV)

[17] *"For our light affliction, which is but for a moment, worketh for us a far more exceeding and eternal weight of glory;* [18] *While we look not at the things which are seen, but at the things which are not seen: for the things*

which are seen are temporal; but the things which are not seen are eternal."

Our God says, "Hold My Hand and Walk with Me!" In these times we are experiencing, are you prepared to do this, Saints? **I leave you with this scripture:**

Revelation 21:3–5 (KJV)

³ "And I heard a great voice out of heaven saying, 'Behold, the tabernacle of God is with men, and he will dwell with them, and they shall be his people, and God himself shall be with them, and be their God. ⁴ And God shall wipe away all tears from their eyes; and there shall be no more death, neither sorrow, nor crying, neither shall there be any more pain: for the former things are passed away.' ⁵ And he that sat upon the throne said, 'Behold, I make all things new.' And he said unto me, 'Write: for these Words are true and faithful.'"

God Bless!

GOD YEARNS FOR A RELATIONSHIP WITH HIS CHILDREN

Saints, all of us are aware of **Revelation 3:20** sharing the fact that our Savior stands at the door of unbeliever's hearts eager to begin a relationship with them. However, our God also stands at the hearts of re-born believers as well, waiting to have a relationship them.

Sadly, many who have given their lives to Christ have not taken the next steps of beginning or strengthening their relationships with God. Saints, the first step is in surrendering to Christ, yet there is much more and many more steps that will draw you closer to our Lord.

Our Lord stands in wait for His children to take these steps. After all, our Lord has just delivered us from the very pit of hell by sending His Son to be the propitiation for our sin and yet many whom have accepted what was done on the cross for them continue to worship other idols, continue to carry hatred, or simply remain "pew riders" in their churches! What if they were to go to heaven today, and at the gates of heaven the angel would ask, "How many people have you won to Christ since your re-birth?" Ouch!

🪙 NUGGET ONE

Saints, this certainly is not new. In the Old Testament, the Israelites had been delivered from captivity and had experienced many graces from God on their journey to the Promised Land! God had fought many of their battles and had certainly demonstrated His loving mercy to them at every turn, including in judgment!

Yet, they too turned from God and found themselves back in Egypt worshipping idol gods and looking to the Egyptians to fight their battle with the Assyrians. Turning their backs on God and His yearning for a relationship with them. They even refused to listen to the prophets God sent to them.

Had God not proven to be a good Father who loved, protected, and delivered them? Delivered them from the very place they returned to seek help and worship their Gods!

🪙 NUGGET TWO

Ah, but Saints, none of us can legitimately point fingers at the Israelites for each of us has turned our backs to our God too at some point in our walk with Him. Perhaps in our prayer lives refusing to always take everything to our Lord? Perhaps our relying on man to fight our battles too, such as doctors or government or friends? Perhaps refusing to hear from God's ministers who are bringing the Word from God to them by not going to church.

All the while, our Father is waiting for us to turn to Him, the one who has delivered us through the blood of His Son!

By the way, the Egyptians had already lost to the Assyrians earlier, one hundred miles from their own border. That only proves that no one can guarantee victory but our Heavenly Father. Time and time again, He has delivered His Children who call upon Him with a pure heart! He has confounded doctors and their diagnoses, bankers and their rejections to His children. So why turn to anyone else, Saints?

God told Isaiah to give a message to these Israelites who turned from Him and looked to idol gods and sought man for help:

Isaiah 30:18–19 (KJV)
[18] "And therefore will the LORD wait, that he may be gracious unto you, and therefore will he be exalted, that he may have mercy upon you: for the LORD is a God of judgment: blessed are all they that wait for him. [19] For the people shall dwell in Zion at Jerusalem: thou shalt weep no more: he will be very gracious unto thee at the voice of thy cry; when he shall hear it, he will answer thee."

Saints, is God waiting on you to turn to Him and take the next steps of building a relationship with Him after he has now delivered you too? Many Saints will give their lives to God and be re-born only to delay going the next step of solidifying a merciful, loving, and grace-filled relationship with Him. Many will sit in church for years as new born Christians before they take the next step!

Should Isaiah be giving you this message? How many souls have you won for the Kingdom, Saints, since your re-birth? Yes, you opened the door, but have you opened your heart? Have you cried out to the Lord, Saints? SELAH!

God Bless!

NUGGETS TO LIVE BY

HOW WELL DO YOU REALLY KNOW GOD?
Exodus 3:1–14

I remember some years ago as a little boy, my mother buying a spice rack. It sat on our kitchen counter and sometimes in the middle of our kitchen table. That is where I used to get into trouble for spinning it. I don't know why I did this ... perhaps I was bored?

It had numerous little bottles all looking the same but had different names of different spices on them. I only recognized two, the salt and the pepper. It was not until recently that at age sixty-one that I realized why I did this. God, I think has a sense of humor sometimes.

Imagine with me for a moment: While looking at my mom, my wife, and the ladies of our church create scrumptious, mouthwatering meals in their kitchens, it is truly a sight to behold. More to our point is how they master these spice racks as they seem to know each bottle and each spice. Not only that, but how each bottle is pulled off the rack to help make each dish delectable ... wow, I am getting hungry thinking about it!

My point is that when we take a moment to ask ourselves, *"Do we really know God?"* — would you be like those who can go to the spice rack and have the knowledge of every spice for every serving of food? Do you know God well enough to know that He can meet every need and which attribute of God will be helpful to meditate, pray, and rest on?

Or are you limited in your knowledge of God which causes you to have limited power as a result. For example, how many only know Him as Jehovah-Rapheka or Rapha (Healer) but not as Jehovah-Shalom (who sanctifies you). Or know him as Jehovah-Elohay (my shepherd) but not as Jehovah-Jireh (my provider).

Our text finds us at the burning bush with Moses being called by God to go to Pharaoh on behalf of the Israelites to deliver them. After God had promised Moses that He would be with him, Moses asked another question.

Moses asked God, when he told the Israelites that God sent him to them to deliver them from Pharaoh, who he should say had sent him. Imagine what appears as irony but may be understood to be the result of four hundred years of what seemed unanswered prayer. As a result, many of the Israelites began to worship idol gods of that time.

Joshua 24:14 (KJV)
14 "Now therefore fear the LORD, and serve him in sincerity and in truth: and put away the gods which your fathers served on the other side of the flood, and in Egypt; and serve ye the LORD."

Now before we look at our Father's answer, it is important to know that in those days a person's name had significance to the character of the individual and or the time in which it was given. For example, Moses' name meant "drawn out of water," for obvious reasons. Even Moses' first son, Gershom, means "stranger in a strange land," as Moses found himself when his son was born.

Now we can see that our Father's answer has significance to what the Israelites needed to know at that time about the character of God. An answer they could understand. As our Father said simply, **"I AM THAT I AM" (KJV).**

It is important to note that God is naming Himself while other gods are named by man! He said further, **"Say unto the children of Israel, I AM hath sent me unto you."**

Our Father was referring to a glorious attribute of Himself that we all must understand before we are to understand anything else about Him. That He alone is sovereign! The Israelites had to know God as sovereign before they could know Him as their deliverer!

That God has no beginning and no end. That our God is complete and sufficient for all that we can ever need. That he is the entire "spice rack"! There is no failure in Him! That God is always in control, never out of control! Pharaoh thought he was in control for four hundred years! That his plan was working . . .

NUGGET ONE

Wait on the Lord, recognize Him as sovereign **(Isa. 40:31)**. Even today we have those who think they are in control. That their plan of abusing the poor and God's people by fighting to deny them healthcare and denying unemployment benefits as they themselves go home to food and medical services is working. But the Great "I AM" tells us to just hold on, He alone is sovereign and knows what we require. He is watching and will provide and not forget!

NUGGET TWO

Understanding the significance of praying for God's will no matter the circumstance as we approach our sovereign God. Just as

Moses was warned when coming before God at the burning bush that he was on holy ground before the great "I AM," we too are to realize that when we approach the great "I AM" in prayer that **He alone stands sovereign!** That to Him alone we are to offer our prayers for He is complete and requires no help! That through the blood of Jesus we are standing in prayer before a complete God. Who knows before we pray all of our needs! Why pray to anyone else?

That He requires no suggestions from us on how to answer our desires. Instead once we realize His sovereignty, we understand that we are to approach Him humbly knowing that His will for us is paramount and that all good and perfect gifts come from Him!

James 1:17 (KJV)
17 "Every good gift and every perfect gift is from above and cometh down from the Father of lights, with whom is no variableness, neither shadow of turning."

As God's children, *if we do not first embrace the sovereignty of the great "I AM," we will not be able to understand the other bottles in the spice rack!*

God Bless!

GOD'S DEEP AND RICH WISDOM
Romans 11:33–36

Now we come to the area of our Father's deep and rich wisdom and knowledge. Paul writes in **Romans 11:33**, *"O the depth of the riches both of the wisdom and knowledge of God!"* However, it is important for us to know that wisdom and knowledge are two different attributes of God as we search to seek whether we really know God.

For example, today many of us know or have known someone who has a lot of knowledge but lacks wisdom. The mature folks use to say, "So-and-so got a lot of smarts but not a lick of common sense!"

A writer wrote, "Wisdom builds, understanding establishes, and knowledge fills." **Proverbs 24:3** says it this way, *"Through wisdom is a house built; and by understanding it is established."*

When we look at the wisdom of our Almighty Father, we must first realize how He built everything and put everything together perfectly. **Isaiah 40:12–14** reminds of the awesome wisdom of God by His creation.

The Isaiah text paints a portrait of God's divine knowledge and His amazingly inimitable wisdom, as wisdom is the application of knowledge. The text reveals that the waters of the earth and universe are like a drop in the palm of His hand. That the entire universe and all of its inhabitants, stars planets, etc., measure the width of his hand! That he alone knows the weight of all the dust, mountains, and hills!

Man is trying to undermine and sabotage God's unmatched wisdom of creation by inaccurately introducing the assertion that two rocks collided. Thus, attempting to eliminate our Father and His wisdom!

However, I always refer them to Luke 19 when Jesus was entering Jerusalem and the unbelieving Pharisees were intent upon stopping believers from praising Jesus. Jesus gave a response that is appropriate even today to "rock believers." In verse 40 he said to the unbelievers, *"I tell you that, if these should hold their peace* (believers praising Him), *the stones would immediately cry out (praises)!"*

Nehemiah 9:6
"Thou, even thou, art Lord alone; thou hast made heaven, the heaven of heavens, with all their host, the earth, and all things that are therein, the seas, and all that is therein, and thou preservest them all; and the host of heaven worshippeth thee."

My friends, God's divine wisdom is revealed in His creation! Even His creation worships Him! Establishing and confirming that God is greater than His creation! "Rock worshippers" must be careful and seek the Creator not the creation!

When one starts worshiping the creation he credits God's divine wisdom to inanimate objects then eventually to himself . . .

In looking at Genesis, we see that each day when God finished His creation He looked at it and said that "... *it was good!*" However, when God breathed life into man and made man a living soul he said, "... *it was very good!*" You see, rocks can't do that! Evolution can't do that, because only God's wisdom can make his creation and creatures so perfectly. To deny creation is to deny the wisdom of God!

God, in all His wisdom, also had a plan for man. More specifically a plan for each of us ... you and me! The Bible reminds us that he knew us before the foundations of the world!

Job had to realize this during His trial. A trial that many men would have a tremendous difficulty to endure without God. God had to tell Job twice to "... *gird up now thy loins like a man ...*"

God had a plan for Job. He had to reveal to Job His wisdom that was larger than whatever Job was facing and whomever Job was listening to, even Job's friends and wife.

God said to Job while Job was whining, "When was the last time you hung a moon in the sky?" (paraphrased). Job finally realized that God's wisdom was far better than man's and he humbled himself in **Job 42:1–6**. In verse 5 he said that he had approached God because he had heard of God by the hearing of his ear, meaning that he had not grown to know God spiritually or knew of His wisdom.

Friends, many of you may only have heard of God by the hearing of your ear. Many may sit in their churches week after week but never understand the true meaning of the wisdom of God. Insofar as His wisdom, is this bottle well known by you on His Divine spice rack?

Job finally said, "... but now mine eye seeth thee. 6 Wherefore I abhor myself and repent in dust and ashes."

Job finally placed the wisdom of God on His divine spice rack and repented for his actions which revealed his lack of understanding to the point that he detested himself.

My friends, do you really want to truly know God? Do you really want to add his wisdom to your divine spice rack? Do you know how?

James 1:5 (Amplified Bible)
"If any of you is deficient in wisdom, let him ask of [a] the giving God [Who gives] to everyone liberally and ungrudgingly, without reproaching or faultfinding, and it will be given him."

NUGGET ONE

Humble yourselves, my friends, and ask with an open heart to receive! Put God's wisdom on your divine spice rack!

God Bless!

GOD'S DEEP AND RICH KNOWLEDGE
John 2:23−25 & Psalm 139:1−3

As we continue to explore whether we really know God, we have reflected on our heavenly Father as having deep and rich wisdom, to now His deep and rich knowledge **(Rom. 11:33–36)**.

Many of us know and can embrace the following facts about God's divine knowledge:
- God knows our necessities
- God knows each of our dilemmas
- God knows each of our hearts
- God's deep and rich knowledge can also penetrate our thoughts and recognize our true character in a way that He will discern our true faith "one by one"!

In our text, we see that many people who witnessed the miracles of Jesus believed! The Scripture specifically says that "many believed"! We see this even in the present day that many profess a belief in Jesus.

However, God's Word said that Jesus' response to their belief was that He "did not commit himself unto them." Why? Is Jesus saying that He had no faith in their faith? That they only believed because of the miracles? Thinking that in believing they could get what they wanted from God?

How many believers profess their faith in God only for what they can get from Him for their human hearts and not the salvation He really offers them for their eternal soul? How many of these same people can read a football lineup and name every player, his stats, position, and jersey number but can't quote the Scriptures in Romans Road or recite the books of the Bible? Ever wonder why games are played on the Lords day? Just saying!

My friends, look at **Isaiah 40:28**, our God is sovereign and Creator of the earth! He oversees all by His deep and rich knowledge and by His knowledge he knows all and is not weary of watching over the earth. He is not only watching over the earth but man's hearts as well.

In our text we see that Jesus did not have faith in the professed faith of these men. Why? Because He knew through His deep and rich knowledge penetrating their thoughts and hearts that their faith would not last. That their faith was only built on what they believed that they could get from God, not what God was offering. This today is the fallacy of prosperity ministry!

John Calvin refers to this type of faith as a "cold faith." What God is looking for, through His deep and rich knowledge, are true believers who will commit to be obedient to Him and follow Him when He calls.

How do we know whether God is only talking to those men of that day or men today as well? In the text God says that He knows "ALL" men and that He knows what is "IN" man! My friend, that means then and now! He further says that no one need tell Him about man! Through His deep and rich knowledge, He knows all about man; after all, He created man!

🧂 NUGGET ONE

This begs the question: is your faith cold? If God takes His deep and rich knowledge today and searches your thoughts and hearts, how will He determine your character? Is it a faith of "What's in it for me?" or is a faith like David's in **Psalm 139:23–24,** "Search me, O God, and know my heart: try me, and know my thoughts: 24 And see if there be any wicked way in me and lead me in the way everlasting."

Finally, the crushing blow to this cold, shallow faith is what Jesus said. That He "did not commit himself unto them." That word commit is the same word as believe that is used in John 3:16, meaning "trust." Some of your Bibles may say trust.

What God's Word is saying here is that because of their shallow, cold faith Jesus would not trust His nature to them—OUCH!

🧂 NUGGET TWO

Those who have a shallow, cold faith, which is in it for what they want out of God only, then God in His deep and rich knowledge will not reveal Himself to them because they cannot be trusted with this knowledge. As we seek to really know God, we must seek Him with a sincere heart and soul being prepared to answer His call when He calls!

Do you really want to know God and all His attributes in His "Divine Spice Rack"? Then I leave you with this Scripture addressed to those who had a cold, shallow faith that followed idol gods instead of following the one and only true God with their whole heart, as some do even today:

Deuteronomy 4:29–31
"But if from thence thou shalt seek the Lord thy God, thou shalt find him, if thou seek him with all thy heart and with all thy soul. 30 When thou art in tribulation, and all these things are come upon thee, even in the latter days, if thou turn to the Lord thy God, and shalt be obedient unto his voice; (For the Lord thy God is a merciful God;) he will not forsake thee, neither destroy thee, nor forget the covenant of thy fathers which he sware unto them."

God Bless!

GREAT IS THY FAITHFULNESS
Luke 2:19

Have you ever had God do something so miraculous in your life that it rendered you speechless? So speechless all you could do was take a deep breath and ponder the faithfulness of our God?

I personally can think of many times where God has rendered me speechless, causing me to ponder His faithfulness in my life. From angels ministering to me at the scene of my motorcycle accident or the joy in my heart witnessing those who genuinely give their lives to Christ in many venues where I have been used by God to present the gospel— from prisons, homeless shelters, Sturgis and other various bike rallies, nursing homes, funerals, and various pulpits. The breathtaking experience of holding my boys (George III, Nicholas, and Nathaniel) in my arms as babies in their delivery rooms. All breathtaking experiences of God's awesome faithfulness!

However, another big moment came from my wife, Willetta. Those who know her recognize that she has an awesome gift of singing. One Sunday morning right before I was to give the sermon, Willetta sang a cappella "He's been faithful." As her eyes were closed I could tell that she was singing that song directly to

God as she had over the years recognized the faithfulness of God throughout her life. A life that has had trials as all of us have had, but this was different. Willetta's heart was singing louder than her voice, if you know what I mean, and all I could do was ponder too of God's faithfulness as she sang! *Been there???*

When she was finished, I stood at the pulpit speechless and just started to pray. Have you ever been there with our God? I want to give **a few nuggets to live by** as we explore the perspectives of the very first Christmas, beginning through the eyes of Mary.

Mary had been told by the angel Gabriel that she was to have a child and that His name was Jesus. That He is the Son of God, the Messiah (Luke 1:35). Mary had to deal with many impediments along her spiritual journey. Some being avoiding rumors of pregnancy before she was married, explaining this to Joseph, his family, and her family! Finally, having to walk to Bethlehem while pregnant as required for the completion of the census. Then being tired and exhausted, she and Joseph were told at the inn that there was no room.

Mary gave birth to Jesus in a smelly stable and while resting there exhausted, came shepherds praising the birth of the Savior, the Son of God. What a glorious sight that must have been! What a celebration! **Luke 2:19** says that this beautiful young woman, Mary, was in such a state that, **"... (she) kept all these things and pondered them in her heart."**

Can you see Mary lying there realizing these shepherds had confirmed what the angel Gabriel had already told her? That as a little girl she had grown up in the synagogue reading about the faithfulness of God to Abraham, Moses, Joshua, Jacob, Noah and the like and now she had realized that He has been faithful to her as well. Saints, that is how we should feel every day and certainly at Christmas! Christmas reflects the faithfulness of our God to send us a Savior that we so desperately needed! It makes one want to ponder this in our heart!

Mary could have also been pondering about the time she walked to see her cousin Elizabeth—where Mary witnessed the baby John the Baptist leaping in Elizabeth's womb, as the baby Jesus entered the room in Mary's womb **(Luke 1:41).**

Luke 1:46–56 illustrate Mary's "Song of Praise" during this visit. This is known as Mary's "Magnificat." In it, Mary praises God as *her* Savior, recognizing that she too needed a Savior (verse 47). She also recognized how God had used her, someone of low estate to show His faithfulness to the world. Indicating to each of us that God can use the lowest and elevate them for His use for His glory! However, there is a requirement . . . **HUMILITY!**

James 4:10
"Humble yourselves in the sight of the Lord, and He shall lift you up."

Mary's "Magnificat" expressed Mary's humility as it was total praise of her Savior and our Savior! All about Him and not about her! Can you see this sweet young woman lying in the stable witnessing the first Christmas, pondering the faithfulness of her savior?

Saints, don't let the hustle and bustle of the commercialization of Christmas steal the pondering in your heart of the faithfulness of our God! Businesses may be worried about their bottom line but we are in admiration of our top line, and that is the throne of Jesus our Savior as we say "Merry Christmas" not "Happy Holidays," because as we ponder these things in our hearts, we can't help but realize that it is much, much more than a holiday . . . It is the day our Savior proved faithful to Mary and to us, His children . . . AMEN!

I leave you with this Scripture:

Luke 11:27–28 (KJV)

[27] "And it came to pass, as he spake these things, a certain woman of the company lifted up her voice, and said unto him, 'Blessed is the womb that bare thee, and the paps which thou hast sucked.' [28] But he said, **'Yea rather, blessed are they that hear the Word of God, and keep it.'"**

God Bless!

HE IS SLOW BUT NEVER LATE

Hold the presses! Hold the presses!
Has Pastor Proctor gone crazy? Calling our Father . . . slow?

Saints, bear with me for just a moment as we will realize that being worldly slow is a whole lot different than being divinely "slow"!

However, you ever wonder why our Savior has not returned yet? To rid Himself of a world that is constantly mocking Him after all He has done for our redemption? Mocking Him with "the new family" which was not ordained by God. Being mocked by the world and ministers who turn their back on God to perform such marriage ceremonies?

The immorality of greed compelling the rich to have a disdain for the poor and the audacity to blame them for their plight to relinquish the rich from their God given commandment to help the poor! Even turning their backs on the poorest of poor in providing healthcare!

Unbelievers scoffing that Jesus is not going to return because there is no God!

Saints, sometimes don't you wish that Jesus would "hurry up"? Thinking sometimes that God is slow but knowing that He is never late!

2 Peter 3:8–10 (KJV)

⁸"But, beloved, be not ignorant of this one thing, that one day is with the Lord as a thousand years, and a thousand years as one day. ⁹ The Lord is not slack concerning his promise, as some men count slackness; but is longsuffering to us-ward, not willing that any should perish, but that all should come to repentance. ¹⁰ But the day of the Lord will come as a thief in the night; in the which the heavens shall pass away with a great noise, and the elements shall melt with fervent heat, the earth also and the works that are therein shall be burned up."

I made the statement over dinner with my wife, Willetta, that "God is slow"! One could see in her eyes that she too thought I was "crazy"! She immediately quoted that "God's time is not our time." I smiled and told her she was all in my sermon and, by the way, CORRECT! She must have a good Pastor!

NUGGET ONE

Saints, we operate daily under time. It controls our lives moment to moment. However, our God does not! Time operates under Him! Hence, we say "slow" but our God says he is not delaying the return of our Savior. Instead our God is "LONGSUFFERING"! Our God is patient with us! He also suffers a long time with us! Saints, mockers say that God is unconcerned about His people, but we know that while we wait for Jesus' return, our God provides! Hence, our God is "longsuffering love"! God's longsuffering love is giving man more time to turn from his wickedness and turn instead to God. God has a desire that all men might be saved **(1 Tim. 2:3–4)**! Ironically, man's claim that our God is slow is good for man.

While "precious" in the sight of God is the death of His Saints (Ps. 116:15), God takes no pleasure in the death of the wicked. God desires that they repent!

Ezekiel 33:11
"Say unto them, 'As I live, saith the Lord God, I have no pleasure in the death of the wicked; but that the wicked turn from his way and live: turn ye, turn ye from your evil ways; for why will ye die, O house of Israel?'"

NUGGET TWO

Saints, God's "slow" equals a longsuffering of love for He desires the wicked to have an opportunity to repent. However, there must be a complete turn from their wicked ways to God! Remorse is good but not enough! It is not enough to be sorry for your sins and wickedness. This is worldly sorrow without repentance or turning to God! In other words, worldly sorrow without repentance has guilt but no real healing power! Saints, godly sorrow is stirred by the Holy Spirit and brings man to complete repentance in turning to God. When man demonstrates worldly sorrow without coming to God, it grieves the Holy Spirit that is drawing him. This is the "longsuffering of love" that our Father endures as this person, while sorrowful and feeling guilt, does not turn to the healing power of our God!

Many times as Pastor, I have witnessed those who are truly contrite regarding their past wickedness, crying rivers of guilt longing for worldly forgiveness never being satisfied because they refuse to come to the longsuffering Healer, our God! My friends, this saddens me! Can you imagine how it saddens and pains our

God? Our God who has provided a way of redemption through His Son for our salvation and spiritual healing?

Saints, he is slow but slow to destroy the wicked . . . thank God! Only by making the complete turn and that's to our God, man will continue to be lost in his wickedness, sin, and guilt! He will continue to be hopeless and without strength. Only God can heal him, and he waits for man . . . for now!

NUGGET THREE

Saints, despite what the world may think about our God, there is a limit to our God's longsuffering love. Verses 10-14 of our text in 2 Peter remind the wicked that our Lord will come as a thief in the night and the verses point out what manner of persons they should be when he returns. Recognizing that the longsuffering of our God is salvation! That they are to be without spot or blemish! That can only be done through the blood of Jesus, my friend! The longsuffering of our God will come to an end and the new heavens will be a reality, and time will be gone and those who have repented from their wickedness and sin and turned to God will be living eternally with our God singing, "Holy, Holy, Holy" to the "ON-TIME GOD!"

BUT it does not stop there, for our God is longsuffering for His believers too! He is warning us too that the "end of all things is at hand . . ."

Saints, are you prepared?

I leave you with this Scripture, **1 Peter 4:7–11** written to believers:

"But the end of all things is at hand: be ye therefore sober, and watch unto prayer. And above all things have fervent charity among yourselves: for charity shall cover the multitude of sins. Use hospitality one to another without grudging. As every man hath received the gift, even so minister the same one to another, as good stewards of the manifold grace of God. If any man speak, let him speak as the oracles of God; if any man minister, let him do it as of the ability which God giveth: that God in all things may be glorified through Jesus Christ, to whom be praise and dominion for ever and ever. Amen."

God Bless!

NUGGETS TO LIVE BY

IT'S RAINING BLESSINGS FOR GOD'S PEOPLE!

Saints, I remember a few years ago riding with my Christian Motorcyclist Chapter to the Sturgis rally in South Dakota. We took the long, scenic route from Kansas City through the Colorado mountains, entering from the west side of South Dakota to do the work of the Lord of spreading His good news of the Gospel of salvation to those who were lost.

One day it was so hot that the motorcycle ride was miserable. The heat of the day, coupled with the heat of the motorcycles was, at times, overbearing and certainly a drain on our energy. We stopped at this ice cream stand and bought milkshakes, ice cream cones, banana splits, and whatever to relieve our misery from this heat.

As I stood at the counter, I happened to see a water hose attached to the building. I look at the attendant and asked her if she would mind if we played with it for a moment. To my surprise and gratitude, she said yes! Saints, we were like kids soaking each other under this hose! Standing there in all our biker gear of leather vests, chaps, boots wringing wet from the blessing of this water on a very hot day!

🪨 NUGGET ONE

Saints, sometimes on the battlefield for our Lord, we can find ourselves in hot, dry places that drain our spirits. We can be amid a trial or circumstance that appears for a time to overtake us so much that we cannot see the forest for the trees! It is in those moments that we must remember the great promise of our Lord: that He will never leave His children or forsake them!

As those who are *"Born of God,"* we are guaranteed that God will provide provision to make it through the heat of all our trials and circumstances. Saints, God may not always deliver us *from* the heat of our trials, but He will always provide for us *through* the heat of our trials!

However, this guarantee is for those who are *Born of God*. The Greek word means those who are regenerated. Those who have been re-born by dying to self and putting on the armor of light offered by Jesus Christ:

Romans 13:12 (KJV)
¹² "The night is far spent, the day is at hand: let us therefore cast off the works of darkness and let us put on the armour of light."

🪨 NUGGET TWO

Friends, not everyone who says *"Lord, Lord"* will enter the kingdom of God. You must be *"Born Again"*! God promises to hear the prayers of those who are genuinely *"Born Again."* Those who have decided to take off their cloak of sin and darkness and turn to Christ and the life He offers that is the light of man, providing direction and purpose through this spiritually hot, dry land we call earth! Providing a rain of blessings for all His children as we make this journey all the way to our ultimate destination which is heaven!

Friends, are you currently in a trial or a circumstance that seems to be draining the very life out of you? Do you feel alone as you are being compelled to endure such a debilitating trial? Your friends offer no help or advice because they cannot be trusted, or they simply do not understand or have empathy?

You seem to be in the wilderness of this heated trial alone? My friend, God does not desire that you be alone. He desires that you turn to Him. He alone will make provision for you to overcome any trial and circumstance if only you will trust Him. If you are in this wilderness, look at what our Lord says to those who are *"Born Again"*:

Isaiah 41:17–20 (KJV)

[17] "When the poor and needy seek water, and there is none, and their tongue faileth for thirst, I the LORD will hear them, I the God of Israel will not forsake them. [18] I will open rivers in high places, and fountains in the midst of the valleys: I will make the wilderness a pool of water, and the dry land springs of water. [19] I will plant in the wilderness the cedar, the shittah tree, and the myrtle, and the oil tree; I will set in the desert the fir tree, and the pine, and the box tree together: [20] That they may see, and know, and consider, and understand together, that the hand of the LORD hath done this, and the Holy One of Israel hath created it."

Are you thirsty for a new life of purpose and direction and the promise of provision through your trials and circumstances? Are you seeking an eternal life of peace, joy, and happiness? Start now, my friends, and turn to one who patiently waits for you to make the decision to follow Him, who loves you so much that He gave His life for you! If you want to be introduced to Him, feel free to contact me and I will pray with and for you! This will be the best decision that you will ever make and that is to follow Jesus!

Finally, **professed Christians** have you been truly **"Born of God"** by being regenerated, or are you playing with God? Saying **"Lord, Lord"** on Sunday and when you need Him, but calling Satan lord by your living . . . **Selah**! Wondering why your prayers are not being answered . . . **Selah**! Wondering why this promised rain of blessings are avoiding you and your circumstances . . . **Selah**!

God Bless!

NO BETTER HANDS TO PUT YOUR LIFE IN THAN JESUS'

Friends, may I ask a few questions? Have you ever given control of your life to anyone and experienced disappointment and maybe even heartbreak? Have you trusted your personal or professional destiny to the hands of a person, company, or profession only to be disappointed or even left out in the cold? Have you finally come to realize that man will fail you?

Jesus in John 10:28–29 says:

"And I give unto them eternal life; and they shall never perish, neither shall any man pluck them out of my hand. My Father, which gave them me, is greater than all; and no man is able to pluck them out of my Father's hand."

Friends, Jesus will never fail you! When you put yourself in Jesus' hands he will protect, guide, and lead you. He will never leave you alone, and no one can pluck you out of His loving hands!

In **John 18** we see the evidence of the love of Jesus for His disciples. Judas had brought the chief priest and Pharisees to arrest Jesus. Jesus knew they were coming and He was prepared to be arrested. He revealed this by confirming to them that He in fact was the Jesus of Nazareth whom they sought.

Then He said to the chief priest and Pharisees to let His disciples go. Jesus was prepared to die alone and there was no need for His disciples to die.

🥜 NUGGET ONE

Saints, look at the security offered to His disciples! He was prepared to die alone. Our Savior offers the same for us when He took the cross alone for our sins. He stood between the Pharisees and chief priest and His disciples. Saints, He did the same for us by standing between us and our pending condemnation for sin!

Friends, Jesus did this to fulfill His earlier promise that all that His Father gave Him He would not lose. He even protected Peter who drew his sword and cut off the ear of the servant of the high priest.

🥜 NUGGET TWO

Friends, look at the protection our Savior provided for His disciples! Before He died for them, He made sure to protect them and lose none. My friends, He can do the same for you today! Jesus offers eternal salvation for those who accept the atoning work done on the cross. Those who surrender their lives into the hands of Jesus! There is no better place to be my friend, for no one can ever pluck you out of His hands! Hands that provide security and protection from condemnation. Hands that desire to lead you all the way to Heavenheaven. Hands that make it possible for you to be called the sons and daughters of God!

John 1:11–12 (KJV)
"He came unto his own, and his own received him not. But as many as received him, to them gave he power to become the sons of God, even to them that believe on his name:"

Friends, our Savior was determined to take the cup of God's fury for the sins of mankind! That we as Saints could rest in His hands. Never to be separated from our God again through sin. Never to be plucked out of His hands.

The cup that was a cup of fury for sin is now a cup of salvation to those who believe and surrender their lives to the hands of our Savior Jesus Christ!

Are you ready to surrender your life into the hands of the Savior? Do you feel our Father drawing you to Jesus?

I leave you with this Scripture:

Psalm 116:12–13 (KJV)
"What shall I render unto the LORD for all his benefits toward me? I will take the cup of salvation and call upon the name of the LORD."

God Bless!

NUGGETS TO LIVE BY

ONE ON ONE WITH OUR FATHER

Saints, as an executive with several companies prior to being called to be a full-time Pastor, I held periodical "one-on-ones" with my staff. During these one-on-ones, my staff member and I would have an open discussion on the goals of the company as it was perceived by that staff member, and goals were tailored for that person to meet those goals.

I am reminded of this as we have found ourselves this past Sunday throughout the area compelled to cancel church services due to the poor weather conditions. Sadly, many would see missing church services as an opportunity to watch TV, get caught up on "honey-dos," or stay in bed.

Yes, Saints, **Hebrews 10:24–25** says, *". . . let us consider one another to provoke unto love and to good works: Not forsaking the assembling of ourselves together, as the manner of some is; but exhorting one another: and so much the more, as ye see the day approaching."*

NUGGET ONE

Saints, I believe that when our Father allows conditions that prohibit His people from worshipping together, He is looking to have a one-on-one with each of His Saints! To have an open discussion with each of us to review the goals and callings He has placed on each of us. Also the goals and callings that He has given each of us for the church and the work of the ministry.

Instead of taking cancelled corporate worship time to sit in front of a television, get caught up on "honey-dos," or stay in bed, our Father wants to meet with each of us individually. We are to use this time that He has made available to us to stand silent before Him in prayer. A prayer where we come to the meeting with open spiritual ears to listen. A prayer where we also come to the meeting with an open heart to take what our Father says and engrave it right there.

Habakkuk 2:20 (KJV)
"But the LORD is in his holy temple: let all the earth keep silence before him."

This is a time that we can stand one on one before God, humbly listening and seeking direction! Saints, imagine the conversation each of you could then have with your pastors after meeting with our Father, one on one!

NUGGET TWO

Yes, it can be hard to meet alone with our Father due to distractions. Going into our closets humbly, not taking any request but humbly listening and seeking direction can be welcomed by many distractions from Satan himself. Jesus experienced this when He sought His one-on-one with His Father, God! Satan tempted Jesus during the forty days Jesus was in the desert; however, Jesus rebuked Satan by the Word of God and remained focused!

Jesus also went into a mountain after the Jews sought to

make Him king to have another one-on-one. Before choosing His disciples, He went to the mountainside all night for His one-on-one. At the death of John the Baptist, Jesus went on a boat alone for another one-on-one! Saints, on many occasions Jesus left His disciples to go away to a secluded place to be alone for a one-on-one with God the Father!

Others, such as Moses in **Exodus 33,** pitched a tent outside the camp to have his one-on-ones alone with God. Elijah in **1 Kings** went into a cave and spent the night to be alone with God for his one-on-one.

Yes, the more we see the day approaching for the return of our Savior, we must come together in worship, but our Father longs for one-on-ones from each of us! When was the last time you went to your one-on-one, taking nothing but an open heart and open ears? When was the last time you shared with your church or pastor what God said to you for the work of the ministry?

Saints, snow days are one-on-one opportunities! Imagine, Saints, if your loved ones witnessed your prayer life of seeking a one-on-one with God during these times of your church being forced to cancel services. They may do what Jesus' disciples did to Him as they witnessed His seeking one-on-ones with God:

Luke 11:1–2 (KJV)
"And it came to pass, that, as he was praying in a certain place, when he ceased, one of his disciples said unto him, 'Lord, teach us to pray, as John also taught his disciples.' And he said unto them, 'When ye pray, say, Our Father which art in heaven . . .'"

God Bless!

NUGGETS TO LIVE BY

OUR GOD FORGIVES . . . DO YOU? (PART 1)
Matthew 18:21–22

Many times, I have been asked similar questions as this involving forgiveness:
- How many times should I forgive someone for the same injustice to me day after day?
- Should I forgive someone who does not want nor seek forgiveness?
- Should I forgive someone who does not deserve to be forgiven?
- Should I wait until they forgive me first?

Many of you while walking your Christian journey here on Earth may yet ask some of these same questions. Then while kicking the dirt beneath you with reluctance, come to an epiphany and with finger pointing say: "My God says to forgive you, but I won't forget!"

Whenever I am reminded of this subject of forgiveness one life-changing event always comes to my mind. It was of a friend who is a member of our Motorcycle Association who happened to be with us as we were going on a mission at a prison here in Kansas. I was to bring the message to several pods as we held a cookout and prayer service. My friend asked to speak with me as we were entering the gates of the prison, and I noticed that he was troubled.

He shared with me that one of the inmates was the one who shot and killed his son close range in the face. I could tell earlier as we were on our way to the prison, riding our motorcycles, that he appeared to be preoccupied. I now realized that he was being convicted by the Holy Spirit to forgive this inmate when he saw him later that day.

Later, as I was giving the message, I looked over and witnessed my friend speaking to an inmate, and later, as I looked over again, they were hugging! My friend's testimony was that of obedience to the Holy Spirit that brought about such freeing relief. The relief of carrying a weakening burden of unforgiveness that did nothing but cripple him. Now he had been relieved and drawn closer to God by his obedience! What a testimony, saints!

I am sure that we all hope and pray not to be tested in such a way. However, one must ask another question as a child of the Most High. How does a Christian reach this point in their Christian walk? What can we learn from God and His Word? First, our God forgives and **FORGETS**!

Hebrews 10:16–17

"This is the covenant that I will make with them after those days, saith the Lord, I will put my laws into their hearts, and in their minds will I write them; And their sins and iniquities will I remember no more."

Psalm 103:12
"As far as the east is from the west, so far hath he removed our transgressions from us."

In our Matthew text, Peter in his wisdom asked, *"How often shall my brother sin against me and I forgive him?"* Keep in mind by Peter saying "brother," he was speaking of a fellow believer. I can just see Peter thinking that the number seven biblically means completion. That at number eight, he would be free from having to forgive!

Jesus gave an awesome answer when He said, *"seventy times seven"*—meaning until eternity. Think about it: if you do not forgive your fellow Christian brother here on Earth, imagine life in heaven eternally carrying the burden of unforgiveness! What will one do while walking down "Gold Street" and see that person coming toward them? Cross the street to the other side. That would be a terrible heaven to live in for eternity! Now I know that is impossible, thank God, as this disobedience to forgive will be the cause of our sins not to be forgiven by our Heavenly Father!

Matthew 6:14–5
"For if ye forgive men their trespasses, your heavenly Father will also forgive you: But if ye forgive not men their trespasses, neither will your Father forgive your trespasses."

Saints, again I ask you, how can one do this? Saints, the answer is simply who is in the driver's seat of your Christian life?

NUGGET ONE

One must consider who is really in the driver's seat of your life. If you are driving, that means that you are driving in the flesh and have no power to forgive, much less forget. Continuing to drive down a powerfully draining path of disobedience to our Heavenly Father! Testing whether He will yet forgive you despite His Word! My friends, that road can only dead end in despair, ulcers, heartache, and a burden that will choke the life out of your Christian walk!

However, when you switch seats with the Holy Spirit, your forgiving becomes a powerful Spirit of forgiveness. Forgiveness that is given under the power of the Holy Spirit who is driving your life ... not you. There is no way that my friend could look at his son's killer and forgive him under his own power. He needed to be obedient to the leading of the Holy Spirit ... no other way! Galatians 5:22-26 reminds us that the fruit of the Spirit among other things is "... temperance, peace, longsuffering, faith, gentleness ..."

NUGGET TWO

The reward for forgiving is to be forgiven by our Heavenly Father! The payment for not forgiving is to be not forgiven by our Heavenly Father ... 'nuff said! If you are not forgiving, the question is who is driving in your life and are you a child of God?

I leave you with this Scripture:

Romans 8:14
"For as many as are led by the Spirit of God, they are the sons of God."

God Bless!

OUR GOD FORGIVES ... DO YOU? (PART 2)
Matthew 18:23–27

This portion of Jesus' answer to Peter involves man's need to understand God's grace as it relates to His Saints in their commandment to forgive in order to be forgiven.

We see that the king represents the King of Kings, our Heavenly Father! Our Father begins by *"taking account of His servants"* (v. 23). To understand this, one must look at the one who was brought before Him. This man oversaw a province for the king and was held responsible for it. This was a very important responsibility given to this man by the king.

The king began by "reckoning"—meaning that he was calculating what the man was doing with the responsibility or blessing that was given him.

NUGGET ONE

Saints, we too have been given a responsibility and a blessing by the King of Kings! That blessing is life! Our reckoning comes first at conversion and throughout our Christian walk. We are called before the King of Kings daily. How are you doing with the life He has blessed you with?

> **1 Corinthians 11:31–32**
> **"For if we would judge ourselves, we should not be judged. 32 But when we are judged, we are chastened of the Lord, that we should not be condemned with the world."**

Yes, the King takes account and reckons what we are doing with the life he has blessed us with, but we must reckon this ourselves daily. Are you reckoning each night before going to bed? Whether you have glorified our God that day? Have you asked Him to reveal and forgive anything that you have done that day that did not glorify Him? Remember, it is not promised that we will wake up on this side in the morning, saints!

I am reminded of a dear friend of mine who requested I speak at his funeral. He was involved in what he thought at the time was a life-threatening accident. He told me that as he lay there on the ground wounded, he looked up to the Lord and simply asked God if he had lived a life that glorified Him. Saints, God sent someone who saved his life that day as he was taken by helicopter to the hospital. His testimony was that God had given him more opportunity to glorify Him with his life!

NUGGET TWO

Saints, we see in our text that it says this man *"was brought"* to the king to settle his debt. As we walk this Christian journey, we are brought to the King of Kings in many ways today. Our Father's Word as we read it will bring us to Him, amen! Sometimes you can read a particular text as you study or listen to a sermon and it will convict you in such a manner you have to stop and go to the King in prayer and praise Him . . . Amen! Sometimes the Holy Spirit will convict you and bring you before the King of Kings as well! What about someone's testimony? My friend's testimony as he lay there thinking he was dying took me to the King of Kings as well! Hopefully some of you even now . . .

My friends, what are some of the things that our King will calculate or reckon in the life He has given you? Will it be your prayer life? Will He look at your spiritual phone bill only to see that you don't show any calls to Him except when you need something or once a week? Whether you are praying for your church, your Pastor, and even your enemies . . .

Will He reckon your commitment to the ministry work in your church? What will he see? Will He see that you have put worldly gods before Him? Are you missing ministry opportunities with your church for selfishness, football, NBA, or March Madness? Will he look at a list of people who you refused to forgive even though he has forgiven you?

My friend, Jesus is letting Peter know in this text that we will all have a reckoning! A "performance report" with the King regarding what we have done with this blessing of life. The question is whether you will come to the meeting prepared to give an account, or will you have to be bound and brought to it, but you will be there!

Praise God in that Jesus is letting Peter know a couple of things that are important and praise worthy for us today! First, we can never pay the debt for sin and lack of service. The man in this text owed a debt of millions that he could never pay. We too owed a debt for our sin and lack of service that we could never pay. That payment was paid on the cross my friends, by the blood of Jesus!

When the man realized that he and his family were to be sold to pay the debt he owed, he begged for patience and worshipped the King, claiming that he would pay!

NUGGET THREE

As soon as the man said "I" will pay thee all, he was doomed, and his worship was false. As we will see in part 3, this man was a "professed" believer that did not understand the **GRACE** of the King who eventually demonstrated compassion for him and forgave him of his debt. Saints, are you a professed Christian not understanding that our King of Kings has forgiven us of a tremendous debt that we could not pay? Have you embraced His GRACE in that you have realized that you too must forgive?

Once acknowledging our God's pardon for us, what can be so unforgiveable that would be greater than what God forgave us for? Or are we saying like this man "I"?

Saints, we cannot do this without walking in the Spirit which God has given us. We must forgive by the power of the Spirit, not our own power as you will see in part 3, for that is embracing what GRACE really means to the believer!

Remember this part of the Lord's Prayer?
Matthew 6:12

"... And forgive us our debts, as we forgive our debtors."

God Bless!

OUR GOD FORGIVES ... DO YOU? (PART 3)
Matthew 18:28-35

Now in part 3 we get to as Paul Harvey use to say, "The rest of the story!" As Jesus was talking to Peter He said that, "The servant therefore fell down, and worshipped him, saying, 'Lord, have patience with me, and I will pay thee all.'"

The question becomes whether the king's servant was as sincere about his worship as he was about his desire to receive patience. Also, whether this servant really understood the compassion and grace of the king when he was pardoned of the huge debt he owed.

Let's look at the evidence of this servant. He certainly wasted no time after leaving the king who pardoned him to continue life as usual! Jesus said that the man sought out and found someone who owed him a fraction of what he had just been pardoned. The servant had just been pardoned ten million dollars while this man only owed him twenty dollars! The question again is whether this servant understood the king's grace.

🏷 NUGGET ONE

Saints, Jesus is giving each of us an analogy of the forgiving grace of our Father which offers pardon for all our sins through the blood of His Son Jesus Christ. That pardon is so huge that we could not ever pay the debt ourselves. Also, the result of that pardon is a new life that should be devoted to Jesus who died for us that we should die to ourselves and live for Him! For if we walk in and by the love of Jesus, we embrace our Father's grace and forgive because we have been forgiven! And our forgiving of anything is only a fraction of what we have already been forgiven by the grace of God. halleluiah, Saints!

2 Corinthians 5:15, 17
"And that he died for all, that they which live should not henceforth live unto themselves, but unto him which died for them, and rose again . . . Therefore if any man be in Christ, he is a new creature: old things are passed away; behold, all things are become new."

The evidence of Saints is that we recognize and embrace our Father's GRACE! Many times, one can allow self to stand in the way of this progression. Let us look at the servant again. In verse 28 the servant laid hands on the man and took him by the throat and said pay "ME"! My friends, one of the biggest reasons we lack forgiveness is that we selfishly take actions against us personally, amen? Fighting back by drinking the poison of an unforgiving spirit, expecting the offender to die but instead you die spiritually. The servant put the man in prison over twenty dollars that he took personally, and he remained in a spiritual prison of an unforgiving spirit. We will see that he became worse off because of it than when he started!

Many times, those who refuse to forgive think they are hiding from others their disdain for their brother. However, as Jesus points out, the fellow servants saw this servant's disdain for his brother and they were saddened.

NUGGET TWO

Never, never believe you can hide your unforgiving spirit! Family members and church congregations are not fooled. Families and congregations can be shattered by this unforgiving spirit which presents havoc to its members. Imagine the awkwardness that spirit gives to those who have a healthy appreciation for both parties but fear one may take your Christian actions as favoritism against the other? That is sad and unnecessary! Jesus said they were so saddened that they went to the king. Saints, when we witness this unforgiving spirit within our families and our church, we are to go to the King of Kings in prayer! Praying hard for these people to repent and understand God's grace and in so demonstrate it in their Christian walk. For who is a God like our God?

Micah 7:18–19

"Who is a God like unto thee, that pardoneth iniquity, and passeth by the transgression of the remnant of his heritage? he retaineth not his anger for ever, because he delighteth in mercy. 19 He will turn again, he will have compassion upon us; he will subdue our iniquities; and thou wilt cast all their sins into the depths of the sea."

When the king heard and witnessed the unforgiving spirit of this servant, he was upset. So troubled because he could not believe that his servant was so unforgiving after experiencing the king's grace and compassion. My friends, can you see our Father looking down on professed believers with this unforgiving spirit and being troubled as a result? After all, when we don't forgive, we scar and hurt His Son who died for us!

Jesus uses the word *wroth*, meaning exasperated. That the king was furious and frustrated!

NUGGET THREE

Saints, an unforgiving spirit, especially by those who have seen the forgiveness of salvation, not only infuriates our Father but frustrates Him to the point of delivering those to their "tormentors"! We see this in other parts of Scripture where one has been turned over to the devil, that the flesh may be destroyed, that the soul may be saved at the return of Jesus Christ. Today this can be the poor health caused by holding on and foolishly embracing this unforgiving spirit. Such things as strokes, heart attacks, high blood pressure, etc.! Even their doctors caution them that it is stress that is killing them! No, my friends, in many cases it is that unforgiving spirit!

Jesus summarizes His parable to Peter in verse 35 by saying that just as this king was infuriated so will be "His" Father with anyone who does not forgive from their hearts. He further says that they must forgive, "EVERYONE his brother their trespasses."

Do you think Peter's original question was answered? Has yours been answered? Do you understand and embrace our Father's GRACE? How well do you really know God? Do you need mercy from a merciful Father?

I leave you with this Scripture as we finish this three-part section on FORGIVENESS:

Matthew 5:7
"Blessed are the merciful: for they shall obtain mercy."

God Bless!

NUGGETS TO LIVE BY

OUR GOD IS A CONSUMING FIRE

As we live in grace on this side of the cross, we realize that others longed for this opportunity yet never had it realized in their lifetime. **Hebrews chapter 11** mentions all the faithful that, while longing for the opportunity to meet our Messiah Jesus Christ, never had the occasion yet remained faithful.

We who are on this side of the cross have had the opportunity to meet our Messiah, Jesus Christ, through the realization of His sacrifice on the cross, His resurrection and His Holy Word. Hence, now we live in grace and not by the Law.

As magnificent as this is, it brings us a greater accountability to this grace whereby we live through the compassion of our Heavenly Father! This means that as Saints we will be held answerable to this grace!

Hebrews 12:25–29 and Deuteronomy 4:23–24

Now we will look at God as a consuming fire! This is a topic that is most avoided by many who do not want to be candid about our Father's judgment of unbelievers and His requirement for those Saints who believe!

🥜 NUGGET ONE

Saints, **YES,** our God is loving, compassionate and forgiving! **YES**, He provides, heals and saves! **BUT** our God is a jealous God! He requires our total heart and soul in service to Him! He requires our total commitment, even more so on this side of the cross! As we will see in these Scriptures! Ready?

In the Deuteronomy scripture above, Moses is advising the Israelites to obey God's Word, the Word that was received on Mt. Sinai. That Word was a Covenant between them and God which was not to be forgotten or broken and taught to their children through generations, while seeking and serving God with their whole hearts.

Paul, believed to be the writer of Hebrews, brings it home to us in verse 25 of Hebrews chapter 12. Here he says, *"him that spake on earth,"* referring to Moses. And *"If they escape not who refuse him,"* meaning that there was no escape for those who were disobedient to God's Word given them by Moses at Mt. Sinai.

My friends, this is the cause of all the troubles that the Israelites experienced throughout the Old Testament, and this is the cause of their lack of peace in Israel today!

However, reading further in verse 25 is a phrase that speaks to us today: "For if they escaped not who refused him that spake on earth, much more shall not we escape, if we turn away from him that speaketh from heaven . . ."

🥜 NUGGET TWO

Saints, please pay close attention to a couple of nuggets in this text. One, God's Word is reminding us that no one escaped from God when Moses gave the Law, and second, "MUCH MORE" we will not escape from God's Word or New Covenant given by

God Himself from heaven! That word speaketh is a Greek word Lalounta, interpreted "the voice of God"! Saints, that is Jesus Christ! Saints, there is NO escape for the closed-hearted who reject God's plan of salvation! Rejecting the New Covenant in the blood of Jesus Christ! Rejecting the work done on the cross! Our Messiah's death burial and resurrection for our sins! That is why there is NO remedy for those who die in the sin of disbelief! There is no prayer for them after death. They have made their decision and their end is sure by the Word of God.

Matthew 12:31–32

"Wherefore I say unto you, 'All manner of sin and blasphemy shall be forgiven unto men: but the blasphemy against the Holy Ghost shall not be forgiven unto men. And whosoever speaketh a word against the Son of man, it shall be forgiven him: but whosoever speaketh against the Holy Ghost, it shall not be forgiven him, neither in this world, neither in the world to come.'"

One can be forgiven for sinning against Christ but not against the Holy Spirit! Why? Because the Holy Spirit knows man's heart. It is the Holy Spirit that convicts man of his sin and unrighteousness! To blaspheme the Holy Spirit is to reject His drawing man to Jesus Christ, who alone will offer man justification and freedom from the bondage of sin and unrighteousness through His blood! Hence, to deny the Holy Spirit, this man will NOT be forgiven in this world NOR the world to come, Heaven! Hence, he will NOT enter into the Kingdom of Heaven! For our God is a consuming fire!

NUGGET THREE

Saints, therefore we are to stay on the mission field in our homes, communities, and wherever it has been revealed the need to win souls for the Kingdom! The time to pray and help the lost is now more than ever! Not after their death, that is too late! Are there unbelievers turning their backs on the drawing of the Holy Spirit in your house, family, or community? Are you turning your back? Friends, our God is a consuming fire! He says He shook the earth for a short time from Mt. Sinai, and they did not listen. Now He will shake the earth and the heavens that shakable things will be removed that unshakeable things will remain! What does that mean?

Saints, our Father is talking about our new Kingdom! That the shakable things of sin, unbelief, pride, hate, lacking forgiveness, and all things that keep man from believing in Jesus Christ and His plan of salvation will be burned off and the new Kingdom of God will remain. A kingdom that will come alive with all creatures praising, serving, and worshipping our Father forever! Imagine there will be a fellowship of all believers together, not impeded by sin and unbelievers! Can you imagine even the stars, fowls of the air, rocks etc., will be praising our God?

The entire universe will come alive with fellow believers in praise, singing "Holy, Holy, Holy!" Embracing and appreciating that our God is a consuming fire!

Finally, saints, verse 28: "Wherefore we receiving a kingdom which cannot be moved, let us have grace, whereby we may serve God acceptably with reverence and godly fear . . ."

NUGGET FOUR

Saints, we must embrace and be thankful for the grace on this side of the cross by living victoriously, serving God with our whole heart, knowing that one day we will be in the new Kingdom of God and those things that are "shakable" in this life will not be able to remain. That we who remain will be in fellowship with each other and with Jesus Christ, our Messiah!

I leave you with this Scripture of victorious living!

Philippians 1:21
"For to me to live is Christ, and to die is gain."

God Bless!

NUGGETS TO LIVE BY

OUR GOD IS NOT A MAN
1 Samuel 15:13—25

The longer we walk with the Lord, the more we are convinced of our imperfections. Charles H. Spurgeon in his book *Morning by Morning* says it this way:

> *"Do you not feel in your own soul that perfection is not in you? Does not each day teach you that? Every tear which trickles from your eye, weeps 'imperfection'; every sigh which burst from your heart, cries 'imperfection'; every harsh word which proceeds from your lip, mutters 'imperfection'; You have too frequently had a view of your own heart to dream for a moment of any perfection in yourself."*

However, we continue daily to witness man in his fickle state attempting to claim perfection! We witness this particularly when man attempts to pass fair and equitable judgment on each other. For example, we witness a congressman wanting to deny voting privileges to drug users when it was revealed that he himself was an offender addicted to the same drugs! Also, his initial attempt to sustain his voting privileges in congress!

Probably the most egregious one is a young adult who was determined to have been driving drunk and as a result caused a fatal accident. Due to his disregard of the law three to four people were killed. However, he escaped prison because of a defense ("affluenza") which determined he should not be held accountable because he was rich and was not properly taught right from wrong!

Praise our Heavenly Father that He is immutable and so are His judgments! As we continue to look at the quest of whether we really know God, we now come to His immutable judgment.

In our text in **1 Samuel 15:29**, Samuel had to remind Saul that God *". . . is not a man."* Why? Because Saul had not obeyed God and God's judgment would not be coming from a "fickle" man who could be disputed or changed. We too should not expect God to look at us like a "fickle" man would.

In this chapter we see where God had an awesome plan for Saul. That plan was to make him king over His people. Saints,, you know God has a plan for each of us as well. Many times, we fail to simply ask our Father what that plan is for our lives and trust Him to reveal it to us . . . amen?

But God also had a mission for Saul. Samuel told Saul to *". . . hearken thou unto the voice of the words of the Lord."* In other words, LISTEN & PAY ATTENTION! Specifically, to the voice of the words! That means to God! Not everything you hear comes from God, my friends! Today we "hearken to God" by making sure that what we are listening to matches up with God's Holy inerrant Word . . . the Bible . . . period!

God told Saul to destroy the sinners, the Amalekites and all that they possessed. Instead Saul disobeyed and returned with Agag the king of the Amalekites along with the best of their animals. Saints, when God gives us a mission, ninety-nine-and-a-half percent won't do!

Scripture said that for this reason, God regretted setting up Saul to be king and as a result that plan for him was rescinded. This grieved Samuel such that he cried out to God all night. Friends, when we see loved ones disobedient and turning their backs on our sovereign God, doesn't that drive you to your knees crying out all night to our Father?

Saul's demeanor after his disobedience was so offensive in that he lied claiming to have performed God's commandments when he stood right amid proof that he in fact had not! We see this today with those professing a belief in Christ, but their unconcealed walk reveals something totally different . . .

Samuel reminded Saul that God had anointed him to be king when Saul was ". . . little in thine own sight"—meaning when Saul was a humble man realizing that he needed God.

NUGGET ONE

Today **James 4:10** remind us that we must obey God with humility, recognizing that we need Him every step of the way to accomplish the mission he has set before us. When one walks in front of God instead of God in front of him, arrogance prevails. Even to the point that one can think he can tell God what God needs!

Saul answered as we see many do even today. That he listened to the people instead of God That plan was doomed for failure from the very moment Saul succumbed to it and so will it be for us today! In verse 21 Saul's arrogance insisted he was right in taking this bounty to offer as sacrifice to God. God said, *". . . to obey is better than sacrifice and to hearken than the fat of rams."*

NUGGET TWO

Even today it is better to obey God than to sacrifice to God! In every church there are those who will sacrifice their time and energy in a church ministry but not be committed to that ministry. Complaining and grumbling at every turn all the while thinking that they are doing God a favor! God is looking for a humble spirit with total commitment to those ministries of His church. What pleases God is a heart devoted to obeying Him. **(Matt. 25:31–41)**

NUGGET THREE

God says that *"hearken (paying attention)* ***is better than the fat of rams."*** In other words, you can give your best but that is still not better than paying attention to God's Word and obedience! Sacrifice is important but only when it is brought to God with a heart of devotion and obedience! **(John 12:1–3)**

Finally, God saw through Saul's weak and unrepentant confession to Samuel in verse 25 as Saul asked Samuel to pardon him instead of going directly to God in sincerity. Saints, this is where our God's immutable judgment is revealed as inevitable, irreversible and just!

In verse 28, God replaced Saul with someone ***"better,"*** and that was David because David demonstrated a heart of devotion and obedience to God.

Saints, Saul's decision determined his destiny, My friend, if you do not know Jesus in the pardon of your sins your decision not to know him will determine your destiny! Don't have those who you know that believe come to you as Samuel came back to Saul in verse 35 . . .

God Bless!

OUR GOD SINGS AND ABUNDANTLY MUCH MORE

Saints, the more I have studied, preached, and shared our Father's Word, the more pictures and paintings seem to fall short of the true depiction of God. The more I walk with Him, pictures and paintings miss the mark of really grasping the grace and mercy that our Father personally represents in my life.

The best painting of God is His Word! His Word represents the brushstrokes of a portrait of His character. When I read and study His Word I can close my eyes and see a portrait that is larger than any portrait man can conceive, much less put on a canvas. Saints, that is why our God says that when we get to Heaven we will truly see Him as He is!

Saints, until then I would like to share an awesome picture of God rarely seen, if at all in man's paintings:

Zephaniah 3:17 (KJV)
17 "The LORD thy God in the midst of thee is mighty; he will save, he will rejoice over thee with joy; he will rest in his love, he will joy over thee with singing."

The prophet Zephaniah gives us a portrait of the attributes of our God that is relevant to us even today!

NUGGET ONE

Saints, Zephaniah reminds us that no matter what hardship or trial we may be experiencing, our God is an ever-present help during our trials. That our God is mighty enough to either deliver us from our trials or provide for us during our trials.

God is the only one mighty enough to save us from our sin and redeem us back to Himself. His might is just a part of this as He desires to save all of mankind from sin if only all would believe.

Another part of this portrait is our God's rejoicing with joy over those who believe! Our God will finally rest in His love. A phrase that many have differing opinions as to its meaning.

NUGGET TWO

I believe its meaning is twofold. Saints, when we get to Heaven, God will rest in His perfect love for us without having to deal with sin or rejection anymore, forever. Secondly, we will finally all as Saints be on one accord and at peace with our Father and each other for we will see Him as He is! One can only close his eyes and see this portrait in one's heart and soul. A canvas will not do this portrait justice, only man's heart and soul!

Finally, Saints, God's Word says that He will "joy over thee with singing"!

NUGGET THREE

WOW, Saints! Our God singing? Over each of His children? Over you as a believer? Over me? As far as I know I have never seen a portrait reflecting our God singing. What an awesome day that will be!

Ah but Saints there is much, much more. The word *rejoice/joy* is from a Hebrew word *gheel* meaning to rejoice exceedingly as in leaping in circles of joy.

Saints, imagine our Father so happy to see us arrive in Heaven that He is singing and leaping with joy! Man's portraits rarely, if at all, have Him even smiling. God's Word has Him singing over us, His Saints, and leaping with joy to see us! Close your eyes, Saints, and let God's Word paint this picture in your hearts!

Saints, we will be singing, "Holy, Holy, Holy to our Father! What do you think will be the lyrics our Father will be singing to us?.

Revelation 2:26–28 (KJV)

26 "And he that overcometh and keepeth my works unto the end, to him will I give power over the nations: 27 And he shall rule them with a rod of iron; as the vessels of a potter shall they be broken to shivers: even as I received of my Father. 28 And I will give him the morning star."

God Bless!

NUGGETS TO LIVE BY

OUR HOLY GOD
Zechariah 3:1—5

How does an accused sinner stand before a Holy God?
Throughout Scripture we have seen that our God is Holy. That everything around Him is Holy. In **Exodus 3:5** Moses was told by God to take off his shoes because the very ground that he stood on in the presence of God was Holy. In **Joshua 5:15** he too was told the same in the presence of a Holy God!

1 Samuel 6:20 says, *"... who is able to stand before this Holy Lord God?"* God's holiness demands that we approach Him as Holy. Jesus, when he taught us how to pray, He said *"... Hallowed be thy name.* Even God's name is Holy and should be treated and counted differently than any other name. That is why we should not use His name in vain. So I ask once again, *"Who is able to stand before this Holy Lord God?"*

Our Holy God could not even look upon Jesus when He took the sins of the world on Himself at the cross. Finding Jesus separated from His Father for the first and only time. This should teach us that we cannot go before a Holy God any ol' kinda way!

In **Joshua 24:19–24,** Joshua had to remind the people that they must count the cost of commitment to a Holy God. Joshua says that

God is a Holy and jealous God, unapproachable by sinful man that worships idol gods. Joshua also stressed that they could not even serve our Holy and jealous God in their condition of disobedience. **1 Peter 1:15** also reminding us *". . . be ye Holy for I am Holy"*!

Today Our Holy God!

We can look all the way back to Genesis to see God's sincerity regarding His Holiness. In 3:23–24 we see that Adam and Eve, after sinning, were expelled from paradise. Not only expelled but cherubim were placed at the gate and a flaming sword which turned every way . . . You think God was serious about His holiness? Will man ever learn to be serious about our Lord God's holiness?

Zechariah's fourth vision given to him by our Holy God paints a beautiful portrait of how we can stand before a Holy God even while being accused of being unworthy.

In this text Zechariah saw the high priest Joshua standing before an angel of the Lord (this is Jesus you will see later) and Satan accusing him! The high priest Joshua was to construct the new temple in Jerusalem for worship and bring people to God because in those days people went to the temple to be in the presence of our Holy God (today we have God's presence within the believer by the Holy Spirit).

Satan was making accusations that the high priest was not worthy to come before a Holy God much less worthy of building His temple. Saints, this is a picture of what Satan is doing even to us today. Making accusations that we too are not worthy of approaching a Holy God. Many times, Satan will even try to say this to a believer going through a difficult trial especially when that believer feels he is not hearing from God.

But you say this was a priest and that's somehow different. Saints, look with me at **1 Peter 2:9** which clearly reveals that believers are all priests! A "Royal Priesthood" called to win souls for our Holy God, who took us out of darkness into His marvelous light! We too stand accused before a Holy God just as Joshua. This perhaps is one time that Satan would possibly be telling the truth about our sinfulness . . . Ouch!

So again, *"Who is able to stand before a Holy Lord God?"* Can the answer be found in **John 17** where Jesus prayed for us and said that, *". . . and for their sakes I sanctify myself, that they also might be sanctified through the truth"*?

In order to stand before a Holy Lord God, we must be cleansed of our sins by the truth of God's Word and by the living Word, Jesus Christ! Being separated to God permanently by belief and trusting in His Son Jesus Christ! Also, allowing the spirit to conform us into the very image of Christ!

Saints, let's go back to our portrait in Zechariah verse 2. This is after Satan has made His case against Joshua standing there guilty in a filthy garment of sin. Jesus comes to the rescue and steps in and rebukes Satan. . . Halleluiah! Is this not the one I plucked out of the fire? In other words, there is no more condemnation for Joshua! Saints, there will be no more condemnation for us either who are believers and stand in Christ Jesus, AMEN! **(Rom. 8:1)**

Jesus commanded that the filthy garment be taken away and a new garment be provided. Saints, that is a picture of our Messiah giving us His righteousness after taking away our sins . . . Halleluiah! Not only that, he said to put a turban on his head (fair miter). In the Old Testament **(Exodus 39:30)** these turbans had the engraving "HOLINESS TO THE LORD" engraved on them. Saints, how we stand accused before a Holy Lord God is by the blood of our Savior Jesus Christ ONLY!

Saints, remember that Jesus prayed for our sanctification by the Word of truth and the Living Word. We again see this in our portrait because after Joshua was saved and presented Holy he was given strict orders and so are we!

NUGGET ONE

Verse 7: We as Joshua are saved to "walk in Christ's ways." We are not saved for "business as usual"!

NUGGET TWO

Verse 7: We as Joshua are saved to keep God's charge! In other words, OBEY HIM! In other words, if God says "Go," we . . . you get the picture . . . GO!

God Bless!

OUR THIRST QUENCHER

Are you curious about the meaning of life? Are you curious about what your role is in this life? Are your curious about what happens after this life is over? Friends, do these questions linger in your heart to the point that you thirst for answers?

Friends, our Father knew that we would have such a thirst! Praise His Holy name for He alone is our Thirst Quencher! Not only will He quench this thirst, but He will also reward those who seek to have this thirst quenched!

It was so important to our Father that He spoke about it in Revelation. He did not send an angel, a mediator or anyone else! This message was so essential to His desire to save man that He spoke Himself!

Revelation 21:6-7 (KJV)
"And he said unto me, It is done. I am Alpha and Omega, the beginning and the end. I will give unto him that is athirst of the fountain of the water of life freely. He that overcometh shall inherit all things; and I will be his God, and he shall be my son."

NUGGET ONE

Friends, our Father offers a solution to your thirst that He will give to you freely. He will give you the knowledge of life that He wants for you if only you will trust and ask Him. As the Great Thirst Quencher, He will give you the knowledge and the fullness of life that is in Him, because the knowledge of life in the world can never quench the thirst that is in you.

Friends, God longs for you to know the plans He has for you. Plans to have you aware of the hope of life through the perfection of life through only Him! My friends He knew you before the very foundations of the world. He had plans for you even then.

NUGGET TWO

The Great Thirst Quencher seeks fellowship with you! He seeks that you know the salvation He offers and the complete forgiveness He offers to those that are thirsty for the answers of life!

Our God wants all to know of the blessed hope we can have in Him that assures us of His presence now in this life and eternally! A presence that brings peace, strength, comfort, grace, and mercy in good times and bad times! An assurance that He will never leave us or forsake us . . . NEVER!

Friends, if you just go to the Great Thirst Quencher, He will transform you into a Saint! You will no longer be citizens of this world but true citizens of heaven! You will be sons of our God with an inheritance, which the world can never take from you . . . NEVER! However, friends, God *will not force you!* He is waiting for you to decide if you want this thirst quenched by the fountain of the water of life He offers freely. Or are you content with the world's fountain which offers only water of death and damnation? The choice is yours!

Are you thirsty? Those who remain fearful in coming to God's fountain of the water of life by rejecting His son Jesus Christ and remaining worldly have their inheritance too:

Revelation 21:8 (KJV)
"But the fearful, and unbelieving, and the abominable, and murderers, and whoremongers, and sorcerers, and idolaters, and all liars, shall have their part in the lake which burneth with fire and brimstone: which is the second death."

Remember, our God the Great Thirst Quencher thought this so essential to His desire to save man that He spoke Himself! What an awesome love He must have for us that He reached out to man with his Son and He Himself is speaking to the hearts of man!

NUGGET THREE:
To the Saints!

Praise God, Saints . . . are you speaking to the lost today? How many people have you won to Christ this year? What have you done to populate Heaven?

"Let the redeemed of the Lord say so," Saints!

God Bless!

NUGGETS TO LIVE BY

PERFECT IN ALL HIS WAYS (PART 1)

Question:

Saints, how many of you have realized that our God is perfect and perfect in all His ways?

God's Word teaches us that when God looked upon His creation He said that it was good! More so, when He created man, He said that it was very good! Man is wondrously made but man is not perfect, nor are his ways! God in His perfectness knows that man needs help and direction!

🔖 NUGGET ONE

IF one agrees that our God is perfect and perfect in all His ways then why does man follow imperfection rather than perfection? Head knowledge that our God is perfect and perfect in all His ways is just a start. Knowing and embracing our God's perfection requires two things.

Psalm 19:7–8

"The law of the Lord is perfect, converting the soul: the testimony of the Lord is sure, making wise the simple.

The statutes of the Lord are right, rejoicing the heart: the commandment of the Lord is pure, enlightening the eyes." (KJV)

Our God left man His Word His Word which is the perfect way for man to follow throughout his life. His Word which is flawless, inerrant, and complete. If anyone tells you differently, you ought to run and run fast! There is no need to add to or take anything away from His Word . . . it is perfect as He is perfect!

Therefore, the world is working so hard to take away God's Word and replace it with its own gospel. Blinding those seeking refuge by the lack of knowledge of God's Word!

In **2 Timothy 3:16–17,** God says this about His Word: *"All Scripture is given by inspiration of God, and is profitable for doctrine, for reproof, for correction, for instruction in righteousness: That the man of God may be perfect, thoroughly furnished unto all good works."*

NUGGET TWO

Yes! ALL Scripture is inspired by our God—meaning that it came about by His direction and approval. Knowing that our God is perfect and perfect in all His ways, He knew we needed the direction of His Word for our lives! Hence, he prepared it for even the simple to understand if only we would ask for wisdom before and while we are reading and meditating on it!

Contrary to some beliefs, our God did not write His Word in code for a select few to interpret for man. God knew who he was writing to and how to write it. To infer that God needed to write in code for a few is without scriptural basis. If man does not read it for himself, how will he know if he is being misled? His Word is profitable for reproof, correction, and instruction unto righteousness that man may be perfect and completely equipped unto good works! It is sufficient for taking man through the spiritual "mine fields of life"!

Remember the old war movies where soldiers had to walk through mine fields? Inevitably one would always step on one at his demise or another would sacrifice himself on one for the group. Saints, how many of you as you walk your Christian journey feel you have stepped on a few mines along the way? How would you like to avoid them? The map pointing them out and the correct way through this field could be sitting on your coffee table not being used! It is the Bible, my friend!

Many mines can be avoided if man would just read it for himself. Our God prepared it for all of us to read and meditate on each Word and direction.

Psalm 119:130–131

"The entrance of thy Words giveth light; it giveth understanding unto the simple. ¹³¹I opened my mouth and panted: for I longed for thy commandments."

NUGGET THREE

Our God's Bible harmonizes with God's nature. It gives light and understanding even to the simple. In other words, God inspired it for man's understanding. Look at the awesome picture shown in this Psalm. David is saying that the "entrance" of God's Word gives light! Saints, you must open your hearts and let His Word in, and our perfect God will do the rest! As David says, he opened his mouth and panted longing for the nourishment of God's

Word! Saints, our perfect God wants you to long for and seek His Word. He wants you to take daily time to study, read, and meditate on the Word He inspired just for you. Are you reading it daily? Do you have a specific time daily that you devote to reading and meditating His glorious inerrant and complete Word? Our Savior died that we may have this Word . . .

Some are like the man who was a fork in the road, driving to a destination yet finding himself hopelessly lost. Not knowing whether to go left or right. So, he pulled over to a gas station and asked for directions. When he got back in his car and followed those directions and he found himself still lost! Ironically, he had a road map sitting next to him on the seat of his car!

Saints, we do this in our spiritual lives, don't we? We find ourselves at a fork in our circumstance, not knowing which way to turn. Calling friends, reading self-help books, and spending hard-earned dollars on seminars! All the while the answer is sitting right there in front of us! Our God's perfect, complete, and inerrant Word! Full of direction and comfort . . . yet we refuse to read it!

FINAL NUGGET

Saints, there are only two reasons man will not pick up our God's Word daily. He either thinks that it is too difficult to read and is waiting for someone to interpret it, or he does not trust it! Saints, Jesus' half-brother **James (1:5)** was inspired to write that God will give wisdom to all seeking it liberally and without reproach, if only we ask! Why not ask our perfect God for wisdom? He desires that we know Him and provided to us His Word that speaks of Him. Trust Him to give you the wisdom to understand it before you read it. As a pastor, I too have asked God to open my understanding before I study and prepare messages or before I counsel and so forth. Trust me, you can trust Him to liberally give you the wisdom you need for He is a perfect God in all His ways!

I leave you this Scripture confirming our Father's Word as complete and warning those that attempt to change or add to it:

Revelation 22:18–19

"For I testify unto every man that heareth the words of the prophecy of this book, If any man shall add unto these things, God shall add unto him the plagues that are written in this book: And if any man shall take away from the words of the book of this prophecy, God shall take away his part out of the book of life, and out of the holy city, and from the things which are written in this book."

God Bless!

NUGGETS TO LIVE BY

PERFECT IN ALL HIS WAYS
(PART 2)

Question:
Saints, how many of you have tried our Father and know His Word will never return void? That His Word will do exactly what it says it will do! If only we would trust Him!

In the last nugget, we realized the importance of our Father's Word. That it is perfect, inerrant and complete, written by our Father's inspiration for understanding by even the simple. That our Father would not write His Word "in code" needing an interpreter! That our Father's Word is profitable for doctrine, reproof, correction, and instruction in righteousness!

> David also says in **Psalm 34:8**
> *"O taste and see that the Lord is good: blessed is the man that trusteth in him."*

NUGGET ONE

Saints, it is not good enough to just know the Word. To be able to quote the Word is not enough either! We must be able to have tried and tasted the Word! David is talking about the "treasure of experience" in trusting our Father's Word. We all have a mother, aunt, or grandmother that is an outstanding cook. One when asked to give you their recipe would say, "I can show you better than I can tell you!" Friends, we must embrace this "treasure of experience"! The experience of walking in God's complete Word! When we do this, we realize as David did that God's Word is a lamp of His life, illuminating his path through life and all circumstances from a shepherd to a king! Albert Einstein said, "The only source of knowledge is experience."

There is a marvelous portion of Scripture where David as a king is looking back over his life in **2 Samuel chapter 22**! David is now a wise king and realizes that as he looks back over his life God has brought him a mighty long way from a shepherd to a king. I would encourage you to read the entire chapter as we too that have "tasted" the goodness of the Lord can also say that the Lord has brought us a mighty long way . . . Amen?

We will focus on verses 29–37 as king David has moved from a traditional relationship with God to one of many experiences of trying God's Word. David has come to the realization that through this "treasure of experience" that God is his strength and power! In verse 31 David says, "the Word of the Lord is tried"!

Affirming that trusting in God's Word from a shepherd to a king has proved that God is faithful to those who trust in Him!

NUGGET TWO

Saints, many times we miss these "treasures of experiences" by forgetting to acknowledge them as we go through them. Also, as we get tied up in tradition in our worship and prayer life. How many times can one say they know God by tradition but do not know Him by experience? In other words, we go to church for traditional worship and praise focusing on the "how-to's" of worship (how should I hold my hands in prayer, should I say "amen" when I feel the pastor's sermon; should we hold hands with others when we pray . . .) rather than the deep meaning of worship that can only come from walking with our Lord? One can quote the Lord walking with Enoch but cannot quote when the Lord walked with them to the point He brought them to their knees!

Friends, we must take our worship beyond reason and tradition to the "treasure of experience"! Then we can be able to say and understand David's challenge to "taste and see that the Lord is good"! Saints, I would encourage you to turn off your televisions, cell phones, iPods, etc., and get a notepad, pencil, and a soda or cup of coffee. Now sit somewhere private and list those times that God's Word proved true in your life and brought you through hardship, sorrow, and trials. Those times when you felt His presence and you realized that you were in the very center of His will. Those times when He turned your tears of sorrow to tears of unspeakable joy. Keep writing until you cannot write anymore. Get more paper if you must! My friends, those are "treasures of experiences" that you need to keep with you and add to them as you walk your Christian journey.

Saints, can you picture David writing this chapter of his life without distractions. David had a long life of communing and serving God. He also in this chapter revealed his patience in trusting God. This gave David a much clearer knowledge of God. It also gave David a greater assurance of his knowledge of God, As well as all the attributes of God.

NUGGET THREE

Saints, the greatest way to get our knowledge of God and to really know Him is through the "treasures of *OUR* experiences" with God! Experiences that will transcend tradition and move to a higher level of worship! Where one would not be constrained by ways of worship but motivated to heartfelt sincere worship derived from a greater clearer knowledge of our God! Causing one to hold up their hands in worship and shout "AMEN" from the congregation of believers and holding hands in prayer with fellow believers that have surrendered their lives to a most Holy, compassionate, and loving God!

The way best to do this is to commune, serve, and patiently trust in Him, remembering each personal experience and building upon them daily. Then we will have a clearer knowledge of our God in all matters of our life. In other words, the personal "spiritual spice rack" we started months ago in our zeal to know how much we really know God!

In verse 36 of our text David says, "Thou hast also given me the shield of thy salvation and thy gentleness hath made me great."

FINAL NUGGET

Saints, David in this verse recognizes God's perfection in all His ways! That our God's ways provide gentle care, gentle protection, and gentle love for all those who trust in Him! Following and trusting in God's perfect ways were time-honored, tried experiences that brought David a mighty long way! From a shepherd boy to a king! Are you following our God's perfect ways? Are you serving Him? Are you communing with Him daily? Are you patiently trusting Him? Do you have a visible list of "treasured experiences" with God that you can meditate upon?

Saints, David was so removed from traditional worship that he did not only write about his "treasures of experiences" in our 2 Samuel 22 text, but he wrote a song about it that is now "A Song of Victory," Psalm 18. If you will read it and compare it to our **2 Samuel** text you will see it!

Do you have a song in your heart about your "treasure of experiences"? I leave you with this portion of the song, **Psalm 18:35**:

"Thou hast also given me the shield of thy salvation: and thy right hand hath holden me up, and thy gentleness hath made me great."

God Bless!

NUGGETS TO LIVE BY

PERFECT PEACE

Saints, has the world's situation caused you to become troubled at times? Has Satan and his angels tempted you to do things that are contrary to what Jesus has taught you to do? Has the Holy Spirit in you had to work "overtime" and "feverishly" to keep you focused that you may seek that perfect peace that only God can provide?

Jesus said in **John 14:27 (KJV)**
"Peace I leave with you, my peace I give unto you: not as the world giveth, give I unto you. Let not your heart be troubled, neither let it be afraid."

NUGGET ONE

Saints, there is a perfect peace that has been given to all of the children of God! A peace that will extinguish troubled hearts! A perfect peace that will sustain a troubled heart through its trials and tribulations! A perfect peace that will strengthen troubled hearts to climb the mountains of despair, the storms of trials and defeat, the lure of Satan himself! A perfect peace that when you find yourself at the crossroads of lashing out in anger and retaliation, this perfect peace will have you take another direction that is more pleasing to our Heavenly Father.

In **1 Samuel chapter 1** we find a woman who exemplified a troubled heart and instead of retaliating she sought a perfect peace that could only come from God.

Hannah was one of the wives of Elkanah who could not have children. Peninnah was one of Elkanan's other wives that could bear children and gave him sons and daughters. Every year Elkanah would take his family out of the city to worship and sacrifice unto the Lord. Elkanah would divide the meat to be sacrificed amongst his wives and his children, giving a larger portion to Hannah. The Scripture says that Peninnah out of jealousy scorned and ridiculed Hannah for not being able to have children.

This troubled Hannah so that she did not eat and cried in the pain of this scorn every year! Saints, imagine the troubled heart Hannah had! Ever been there?

NUGGET TWO

Saints, when a troubled heart is at the crossroads that Hannah's heart was in, one may seriously look to retaliate against such a heartless, mean, and cruel adversary. Many of us, male and female, can shamefully say we took that direction at this crossroads many times! However, Hannah did not. Hannah did not run to retaliate or run from her troubled situation, instead Hannah ran to God WITH her troubled situation! Oh, praise God, Saints, what an example of faith!

Hannah was so troubled but full of faith that as she prayed her lips were moving but there was no sound coming from her mouth! Saints, have you ever prayed to the Lord so hard that your heart was talking to Him faster than you could form the words? If you have not, live long enough and you will!

Hannah told the priest who when seeing her thought she was drunk that she was not an evil woman but that she was "pouring out her very soul" to God! Oh, Saints, Hannah was giving it all to God leaving NOTHING behind! Hannah's faithful example caused even the priest to join in her prayer for deliverance. Hannah took her very soul directly to God and the priest joined in without her having to tell him the reason for her troubled heart . . .

God remembered Hannah and answered her prayer. Hannah left the temple at such a perfect peace that she ate and the next day got up early ate with her family, including Peninnah, and worshipped God together! Saints, God gave Hannah such a perfect peace that she could dine and worship with her enemy because she was faithfully focused on God not her trouble or her enemy!

NUGGET THREE

Saints, he can do the same for you and me:

Isaiah 26:3 (KJV)
"Thou wilt keep him in perfect peace, whose mind is stayed on thee: because he trusteth in thee."

God Bless!

NUGGETS TO LIVE BY

3

SAINTHOOD

NUGGETS TO LIVE BY

SAINTS, IS GOD REAL IN YOUR LIFE TODAY?

Saints, is God so real in your life today that nothing can stand between you and God's plan for you? So real, that neither the giant of doubt, fear, or disobedience could stand between you and our Father's plan for you? If you say yes, then God must be real in your very soul today!

Well, Saints, in **Numbers 13 and 14** we witness a lesson that is valuable to us today. God's ultimate plan for those who have given their life to Him through His Son Jesus Christ is that we spend eternity with Him in Heaven! However, while yet here we are to faithfully endure until His Son's return.

In **Numbers 13 and 14** we see God's people at the very threshold of the land of milk and honey that was promised to them by God, and yet they allowed three giants to stand between them and God's plan of the promised land for them! Saints, with Heaven in sight, are any of these giants standing between you and God's promise of Heaven?

NUGGET ONE

THE GIANT OF DOUBT! Even after receiving a report of the land in all its splendor the Israelites still doubted that they could take the land from the inhabitants as God told them to. They looked at the size of the giant's stature and their fortresses and let their doubt stand between them and the plan God had for them.

They looked to their power versus God's power! Even though God by His grace and power had brought them this far.

Saints, have you experienced the giant of doubt as to your salvation? Are you assuming that your way into Heaven is by your works versus the work that has already been done by our Savior Jesus Christ at Calvary? Are you one who believes you can lose your salvation that you did not earn but was given to you by the grace of God when you first believed and surrendered your life to Him through the blood of Jesus and sealed it by the Holy Spirit which dwells in you **(Eph. 1:13–14)**?

Saints, just as the Israelites misunderstood the promise and plan God had for them had nothing to do with their power but His grace and power, we must be careful not to think similarly as to God's grace and power for our inheritance, Heaven!

NUGGET TWO

THE GIANT OF FEAR! Notice *ALL* the congregation of Israelites cried out in fear and wept all night in fear. They allowed the giant of fear of the impossible to stand between them and the plan God had for them. They had forgotten that in their journey they had been delivered many times from the impossible by God. The river Jordan, the Red Sea, direction by cloud by day and fire of comfort by night. Nourishing manna to eat! God had shown them of His grace and power yet they allowed the giant of fear to stand between them and the plan God had for them.

Saints, as you walk this Christian journey how often have you allowed the giant of fear of the impossible stand between you and God's plan for you? How many times, Saints, even though God had delivered you by defeating the impossible in your journey? Such that you stand in awesome praise of His deliverance and then soon forget when another giant of impossibility approaches you!

NUGGET THREE

THE GIANT OF DISOBEDIENCE! Saints, the giants of doubt and fear lead all the congregation of Israelites to the giant of disobedience! Instead of listening to the Joshua and Caleb's warning, they set out to stone them and seek another leader to return to bondage **(Neh. 9:17)**! They had hardened their necks to God's grace and once again sought their own remedy by disobeying God!

Saints, is God real in your soul today? Are you ready to please Him by not doubting His plan for you? Are you ready to not allow fear of the impossible because you have a relationship with the "Way Maker"? Will you remain obedient to God by trusting in Him and not in yourself? Jacob and Caleb put it this way:

Numbers 14:8–9 (KJV)
⁸ "If the LORD delight in us, then he will bring us into this land, and give it us; a land which floweth with milk and honey. ⁹ Only rebel not ye against the LORD, neither fear ye the people of the land; for they are bread for us: their defence is departed from them, and the LORD is with us: fear them not."

God Bless!

NUGGETS TO LIVE BY

SAINTS, THERE IS MORE TO LIFE
Acts 21:13-14

Saints, what are the purposes our Father has for you that must be carried out no matter the risks or circumstances? Requiring you to overcome obstacles that may even involve loved ones and friends who may attempt to alter your course of following our Father's will. Not to mention those enemies that lay in wait to destroy you as you follow His will!

In our text Paul experienced just that! God's will for him was to go to Jerusalem and yet the Holy Spirit confirmed to Paul that he would be bound and delivered to the Gentiles while there doing the will of God. Paul's friends pleaded and shed tears for Paul begging him not to go. Basically, not to do the will of God.

However, Paul confirmed with his loved ones that not only was he prepared to be bound and delivered to the Gentiles but also to DIE in Jerusalem for the name of the Lord Jesus!

Paul's commitment to stand firm and remain steadfast to the will of God was an encouragement to doubters. To the point that they too stopped trying to persuade Paul to avoid going to Jerusalem and said, "The will of the Lord be done."

🪙NUGGET ONE

Saints, does your commitment to stand firm and remain steadfast to the will of our God win souls to God? Or encourage doubters? Paul's commitment and steadfastness are winning souls to our God even today! Paul's commitment to obey God to win souls and worship Him in the name of Jesus would not be denied! Will yours? Or does your will overshadow our Father's? Or are you prepared to die for the will of our God?

These are key questions for us as Saints to understand that there is certainly more to life! Unlike the days of Paul, we are not tested to be martyrs for our beliefs. Being put to death for spreading the gospel! But the question of whether we are prepared to die for the cause of Christ is yet still important to true Christians today!

Imagine with me Paul walking to Jerusalem and with each step knowing that he will be bound and delivered to the unbelieving Gentiles, yet he never turned form his purpose to obey God! Not afraid of his enemies nor being moved by the tears and beckoning of his friends! Taking every step with a willing mind prepared to die for the cause of Christ! What an awesome sight of determination that must have been! I know you are thinking it is awesome that today we do not have to be tested to the extent of being martyrs for following the will of God . . .

🪙NUGGET TWO

Saints, on the contrary; we are required to be martyrs for the will of God. While today we may not be put in prison or hanged for our beliefs, we must be martyrs! For us to embrace the fact that there is more to life we must be prepared to die for the purpose of God. Saints, that enemy that we must be prepared to die to is simply . . . **_US!_** We must DIE to self before we can understand that there is in fact more to life!

Saints, we must be prepared to die to self willingly. Without turning from the purpose of God. Without succumbing to the tears and beckoning of friends to ignore and deny the will of God. Not being afraid of pending dangers and threats that this world will bring to those Saints committed to make every step toward God's will count. Then and only then will we be able to understand that there is in fact more to life! Joshua put it this way in **chapter 24 verse 15**:

> *"And if it seem evil unto you to serve the Lord, choose you this day whom ye will serve; whether the gods which your fathers served that were on the other side of the flood, or the gods of the Amorites, in whose land ye dwell: but as for me and my house, we will serve the Lord."*

NUGGET THREE

Saints, a minister once said that based on **Galatians 2:20** we as Saints are in fact "dead men walking." Those who have fellowship with Christ's crucifixion have died to self and now walk with Christ.

However, I say all men are "dead men walking"! The real question is if you are dead **_with_** Christ or dead **_to_** Christ for rejecting the grace of the cross.

My friends, there are at least two positions that a true Christian can be recognized as "dead men walking **_with_** Christ," signifying the position of the true Christian.

Position One: are you in fact dead to sin and no longer the servant of sin? Yes, we all sin and fall short of the glory of God but the question remains, are you a SERVANT of sin? **Romans 6:6–7** puts it this way:

"Knowing this, that our old man is crucified with him, that the body of sin might be destroyed, that henceforth we should not serve sin. For he that is dead is freed from sin."

Position Two; are you dead to the world and the world dead to you? **Galatians 6:14** puts it this way:

"But God forbid that I should glory, save in the cross of our Lord Jesus Christ, by whom the world is crucified unto me, and I unto the world."

Saints, next week part 2 of "There is more to life!" until then, I leave you with this scripture **Matthew 16:25-26**:

For whosoever will save his life shall lose it: and whosoever will lose his life for my sake shall find it. For what is a man profited, if he shall gain the whole world, and lose his own soul? or what shall a man give in exchange for his soul?

God Bless!

THE POWER WITHIN (CONTINUED)
2 Corinthians 4:6−7

Saints, earlier we discussed the topic of "There Is More to Life." Realizing that we are most powerless as unsaved people seeking to do our will and not that of our Father. Paul demonstrated that we must be prepared to die for the name of our Lord. That death we now understand in **Galatians 2:20** is to self.

Now as we seek to embrace the fact that there is more to life we must realize who is the giver of this life and can rescue us from our death.

John 5:24:
"Verily, verily, I say unto you, He that heareth my Word, and believeth on him that sent me, hath everlasting life, and shall not come into condemnation; but is passed from death unto life."

NUGGET ONE

Saints, the best life is one freely given by our Father through Jesus Christ! A life whereby we have been brought back to peace and harmony with our God. A life where our Father's will and desires overshadow ours as a way of life. A life anchored in God sent by Him through His Son. After all, Jesus *is* the Way, the Truth and the Life! **Colossians 1:17** reminds us that he was before all things and by Him all things consist. Unbelievers, if you want more out of life accept and embrace the giver of life, Jesus Christ. He holds all things together and has a purpose and plan for all those who are His.

Saints, **2 Peter 1:4** assures us who have died to self the promise of being partakers of the divine nature of our Father. Whereby as believers we no longer do things like we use to before our conversion.

2 Corinthians 4:6–7

This text reminds us that we have been given a precious treasure that is within each believer. A treasure that will replace our weak bodies with the power from our Heavenly Father who now dwells within the believer. This is our great and precious promise!

My friends, a precious treasure that will transform us as believers into a more abundant life. A life with enduring power leaving the Holy Spirit to guide us through any obstacle we may have before us. Reminding us that our Father will never leave us or forsake us . . . ever!

NUGGET TWO

Saints, no man can do this for himself. We must realize that we are like earthen vessels . . . weak, that the power may be of God and not of us! Therefore, greater is He (God) that is in us (the believer) than he that is in the world! Praises to our Father who provides this life through His Son, Jesus Christ! The Good

Shepherd that unlike the world seeks to give abundant life to all believers! John 10:10:

"The thief cometh not, but for to steal, and to kill, and to destroy: I am come that they might have life, and that they might have it more abundantly."

This abundant life is demonstrated in the believer's ability to be victorious even through his strife and trials!

Verse 8 and 9 of our text in **2 Corinthians** puts it this way:

"We are troubled on every side, yet not distressed; we are perplexed, but not in despair; Persecuted, but not forsaken; cast down, but not destroyed . . ."

NUGGET THREE

Saints, an abundant life so strong that when it seems like we as the children of God feel like the world is on top of us and we are being attacked from every side we yet have "the power within"! The very presence of God within us! His presence will keep us from distress because He is right there with us. All we must do is lean on Him and not ourselves. Even while Satan himself seems to be working overtime. Knowing that all things work for the good for those who love God and are called for His purpose!

Similarly, we have a reminder of hope within us at those times when It seems we may be amid our dilemma, perplexed and without answers but knowing confidently that our Father will deliver and provide. That is why we have no despair knowing our Father will be there and all we must do is be patient for He is a great and mighty God!

So great and mighty that even when we are knocked down by the world, we are not knocked out or defeated! Because we carry victory in us . . . AMEN!

Saints, before we accepted Christ and died to self, it was all about us and not about our Father. However, once we relent to the Spirit and allow our Father to provide life and life more abundantly, God can now work with us. And this work will begin as soon as the unbeliever accepts Christ and all the way to eternity! Where we will live forever with our Father!

My friends, an abundant, better life through the life giver will keep us now and take us all the way home. Our God was not short of His promises. That promised abundant life here, but also abundant life in the life to come!

I leave you with this Scripture:

1 Corinthians 15:9
"If in this life only we have hope in Christ, we are of all men most miserable."

God Bless!

REJOICE IN THE LORD, SAINTS!
Philippians 4:4

I remember being in the hospital as a youngster back in Chicago. I had just had major surgery and prior to going into surgery my parents were at my bedside encouraging me and what I now know they were also praying for me! Once out of surgery I was going in and out of consciousness while my body was attempting to fight off the anesthesia.

However, I will never forget that each time I awoke both my mom and dad were there by my bed.

In this portion of Scripture, Paul is reminding the Philippians that they are to rejoice in the Lord always. When I read and meditate on this verse, I am mindful of how my parents were there for me as I mentioned earlier. That our Lord never sleeps and while we are asleep he too is by our bedside looking over us and there to wake us up to greet Him in prayer every blessed morning . . . hallelujah!

🧈NUGGET ONE

Saints, Paul in the first part of our text is reminding us that we have reason to rejoice in the Lord *"always"*! From the first time we open our eyes in the morning knowing that when we laid our head down the night before that waking was not promised. To eternal life given to us by our Lord who took our burden of sin upon Himself which we were unable to do ourselves. Therefore, as **Romans 12:12** says, we are to *"rejoice and exult (revel) in hope . . ."!* Saints, when we do this it will cause us to–as **1 Thessalonians 5:16** says:

"Be happy [in your faith] and rejoice and be glad-hearted continually (always) . . ."

This, Saints, is our peace that the world does not understand. A peace that the world does not offer but only comes from our Lord, Jesus Christ!

Then Paul says in our **Philippians 4:4** text, *". . . and **again I say, rejoice.**"* Why would he say this twice? Could it be that sometimes when we read Scripture we can miss the full meaning and purpose of the Scripture? Or, can it be that our Lord is trying to bring your attention to a point that He wants you to be certain of its benefit to us as His children?

Saints, our Lord wants to emphasize that we are to rejoice no matter the circumstances that we may find ourselves in as we walk this Christian journey. Knowing that we serve an ever-present God who watches over us both day and night, amen?

We can rejoice because of our Lord's love and compassion for us that was revealed on the cross of our salvation! Providing the bridge to eternal life if only we would believe on His Son! A love so deep and certain that nothing can separate us as Saints from it:

Romans 8:38–39
"For I am persuaded, that neither death, nor life, nor angels, nor principalities, nor powers, nor things present, nor things to come, Nor height, nor depth, nor any other

creature, shall be able to separate us from the love of God, which is in Christ Jesus our Lord."

🟦 NUGGET TWO

Saints, when we know that as children of light that our Lord's love can never be compromised or taken from us by any means and that He watches over us with His love and compassion, how can we not rejoice continually and repeatedly? How can we fail to wake and not sing heartfelt praises to our Lord? How can we allow anything to steal our joy of rejoicing?

Our very own Deacon Clyde Stepps here at United Missionary Baptist Church has a consistent testimony of waking to the joy of the Lord daily! Isn't that awesome? Isn't that how all believers should wake and go through our day? How many souls could we win for Christ if we did?

If you are certain as Romans says that no one can separate you from our Lord's love, then why does one allow disobedience, holding grudges, television, or laziness to keep them from rejoicing in our Lord?

Once again, a question please: If Jesus came back on Sunday morning, will he have to wake you up, turn your television off, or summon you from a sports game to meet Him in the air? Or will he summon you home with your church congregation as you are worshipping Him and rejoicing in your hope together as a church family?

Will you meet Him in the air with excuses, or rejoicing? Excuses that you may not like the pastor who God sent to you . . . or the congregation, or that God was not more important than the entertainment of the world? Or would you say that you needed your sleep?

Rejoicing in the Lord is what a Christian does when he is sold out on the Lord as the Lord has revealed by the cross that He is sold out on him! There is no doubt that our Lord is sold out on His children, but are you as His child sold out on Him? Are you ready and willing to worship and rejoice in Him every day through every circumstance? Are you ready to stand firm in your worship and rejoicing or fall prey to this world and wonder why you are not a peace?

If you would like to know more of how to reciprocate being sold out on our Lord as He is on you, drop me an email and I will provide you more information.

Until then I leave you with this Scripture:

1 Peter 4:12–13
"Beloved, do not be amazed and bewildered at the fiery ordeal which is taking place to test your quality, as though something strange (unusual and alien to you and your position) were befalling you."

"But insofar as you are sharing Christ's sufferings, rejoice, so that when His glory [full of radiance and splendor] is revealed, you may also rejoice with triumph [exultantly]." **(1 Peter 4:12–13)**

God Bless!

RESTING IN GREEN PASTURES OF EXPECTATION

Saints, on my way to Texas last week to see my new grandson, my wife and I passed many pastures housing sheep. I could not help but be drawn to one of the most memorized portions of Scripture, **Psalms 23.** Particularly verse 2:

Psalm 23:2 (KJV)
² *"He maketh me to lie down in green pastures: he leadeth me beside the still waters."*

The sheep we passed looked very peaceful as they sat there without a care in the world. Then it hit me that they were sitting in fields of expectation! Meaning that all that they would ever need and expect was right there in the pasture. Whether the expectation would be safety, food, and nourishment, love or deliverance from any trial that may present itself to any of them.

In **Psalm 62:5**, David makes it very clear who will deliver on that expectation and how his soul will respond.

🥜 NUGGET ONE

Psalm 62:5 (KJV)
⁵ "My soul, wait thou only upon God; for my expectation is from him."

Saints, David makes it clear that his expectation only comes from God. As sheep we too must realize that our expectations can only come from our God and not man, saints, angels, or anyone else . . . only God!

David's soul will not be moved because he has a very personal relationship with God. Imagine the sheep in the pasture and their relationship with the shepherd. The sheep knew they could count on the shepherd and therefore they rested perfectly in the pasture of expectation. We too are able to be in perfect rest in this green pasture of expectation! How, you say?

David recognized God only as his rock, salvation, strength, glory, and refuge. David specifically says "my," denoting a very close relationship that he has cultivated with God and learned to depend on.

🥜 NUGGET TWO

Saints, the only way we can understand David is to also claim God as "our" God! More specifically, each of you should be able to say with all sincerity that God is "MY" rock, salvation, strength, glory, and refuge, no one else!

First, David says that to get to that point, we must first "trust God at all times"!

🥜 NUGGET THREE

We are not to only trust God in bad times but good times as well! It is just as demanding to trust God in good times as well as bad times. Many times, when things are going great we fail to glorify God and express our appreciation to Him for His blessings towards us each day.

Think about it, Saints. How many of you have children, young or adult age, who only come to you when they have a need and you do not see them any other time? How does that make you feel about your relationship with them and theirs with you?

Second, David says that we are to "pour out our hearts before God." In other words, we are to take all our cares, desires, sins, and sorrows to God only! Because God alone is our refuge, no one else!

Psalm 62:8 (KJV)
⁸ "Trust in him at all times; ye people, pour out your heart before him: God is a refuge for us. Selah."

Worth pondering . . . Selah? Are you sitting in the green pastures of expectation?

God Bless!

NUGGETS TO LIVE BY

SAINTS, ARE YOU STILL ON THE RUN?
John 20:1-10, 30-31 and Acts 2

In this text, we see that John is writing a historically detailed account of Christ's resurrection. Many details that even led John to believe in the resurrection the moment he witnessed what he saw in the empty tomb. John's historical account was, as he said, to help others to believe that Jesus Christ is the Son of God and in their believing they might have life in His name.

John listed many evidences such as he and Peter running to the tomb and made mention that he outran Peter! He mentioned the stone being rolled away. Frankly, that was for our benefit as Jesus did not need the stone to be move as he could have just gone through it as he did the locked doors at the place he met the disciples later.

The placing of the burial garments "wrapped together." Denoting that they were wrapped as if they were yet around Jesus' body, but he was not there! All these evidences could have been enough for an episode of *Forensic Files* and yet there was the final evidence that really tells all of us today the true meaning of Easter!

🪙 NUGGET ONE

We see the evidence in John when he believed, but let us look at Peter. John said Peter stood in the tomb. Let us go back a little. Peter was a man on the run, being a slave to fear because he and the others were being hunted like dogs to be put to death. Saints, there is no real evidence that Peter was even at the crucifixion!

Now Peter stands in the tomb! Saints, can you see him thinking about the things Jesus told all of them such as "Let not your heart be troubled; I go to prepare a place for you . . ."; "I will not leave you comfortless . . . I will pray the Father that He will send to you another comforter . . . that will remind you of all things I have said and teach you . . ."

🪙 NUGGET TWO

Imagine Peter and John pondering on all those things as they looked in the empty tomb. Saints, have you pondered on those things? Have you understood the true meaning of Easter, or are you still "on the run" like they were? Or are you running instead for Jesus?

Ah Saints, the greatest evidence that Christ had risen took place some thirty days after John and Peter stood there at the tomb.

🪙 NUGGET THREE

The disciples had gone to Judea and appeared full of joy speaking in such a way that all who were in the crowd of different languages understood them! The people were astonished and bewildered and said surely these men must be drunk!

Saints, guess who spoke up? Peter who had been on the run, fearful for his life, possibly not even at Jesus' crucifixion, denying Him three times before the cock crowed—stood up and addressed the bewildered crowd! Peter and the rest of the disciples went from "men on the run" to "men on the run for Jesus"! Saints, that is the true meaning of Easter! That is the evidence of Christ's resurrection for the world to witness in you!

Peter stood before those who still sought to kill them, and accused them of killing Jesus but told them that Jesus had risen and was sitting at the right hand of God! He admonished them to repent and believe that Jesus is the Christ. That God had told Jesus that He would make His enemies His footstool. Finally, Peter looked at their accusers and said, "Therefore let all the house of Israel know assuredly that God hath made that same Jesus, whom ye have crucified, both Lord and Christ." **Acts 2:36 (KJV)**

Saints, at that moment about three thousand came to the Lord that day! The most glorious evidence of the resurrection of Jesus Christ is His people! These disciples turned from "men on the run and slaves to fear" to "saints running for God"! Saints, are you still "on the run" or have you allowed the Holy Spirit that Jesus prayed to the Father to give to you comfort, keep, guide, and teach you on this Christian journey? As Saints we are without excuse for not standing boldly for Christ, as we as the disciples have been sealed by the Holy Spirit of our Father, God!

<u>YOU</u> are the evidence of the resurrection to this world that wants to deny it and teach our children and those who are weak that Easter is about a rabbit and eggs.

Hebrews 10:23 (KJV)
[23] "Let us hold fast the profession of our faith without wavering; (for he is faithful that promised)..."

God Bless!

NUGGETS TO LIVE BY

SAINTS, WE ARE SOMEBODY!

Saints, Paul reminds us in Ephesians that by the blood of Jesus we become somebody who once was a foreigner and stranger to God. James, the half-brother of Jesus, put it this way: *"Whosoever therefore will be a friend of the world is the enemy of God" (James 4:4).*

While this world is so preoccupied with putting up walls, protecting borders, separating families, and promoting racial strife, our God has made a way of tearing down the middle wall of partition making us one in Him. Transcending from enemies of God to a new family and a new nation by the blood of His only begotten Son, Jesus Christ.

> **Ephesians 2:13–14 (KJV)**
> *[13] "But now in Christ Jesus ye who sometimes were far off are made nigh by the blood of Christ.*
> *[14] For he is our peace, who hath made both one, and hath broken down the middle wall of partition between us . . ."*

NUGGET ONE

Saints, with this new family comes many things. First of which, the fact that those who have given their lives to Christ are all now Saints! Meaning that we have been set apart to God by the cross. We are no longer citizens of this world but now are citizens of Heaven. Our citizenship has been ordained and sealed by the Holy Spirit of promise which now dwells within us as believers!

Our citizenship will be in a place where no walls will separate us. No one will be separated and banned based on their race or color! No dictatorship but a loving and gracious Father! Ah, Saints, let the world continue its building of walls, separating of families, the rich taking advantage of the poor and the honoring of godless leaders for soon there will be a separation! Asaph put it this way:

Psalm 73:27, 28
"For, lo, they that are far from thee shall perish: thou hast destroyed all them that go a whoring from thee. But it is good for me to draw near to God: I have put my trust in the Lord God, that I may declare all thy works."

Praise God, we are *somebody* moving on up!

NUGGET TWO

Paul further proclaims that we as Saints are **"Fellow citizens with the saints, and of the household of God"**! My fellow Saints that is speaking of the church! Fellow Saints in the same church! No more churches with labels like Black Church, White Church Hispanic Church and so on. Everyone worshipping together our Father in Spirit and in truth! We may as well practice this now for in Heaven we will be doing just that!

Also, each Saint being held accountable to bringing their God given gifts to the church. This is not just offering and tithes but a gift that God has given each to work in a ministry in the church. No one being a pew rider! If you are not working in your church, Saints, you are cheating God out of the gift He has given you to help your household.

How many of you had chores in your house while growing up? We as Saints have responsibilities to our fellow Saints in the household of faith as well, if not more, so for it is ultimately to God that we get to work. It is a privilege to serve our Father for all his blessings towards us, Saints!

Ephesians 4:16 (KJV)

¹⁶ "From whom the whole body fitly joined together and compacted by that which every joint supplieth, according to the effectual working in the measure of every part, maketh increase of the body unto the edifying of itself in love."

Saints, we are *somebody* moving on up! We are all as fellow Saints, family! Let us together dwell in the peace that our Father has set aside for His people. A peace that this world will never understand nor desires to:

John 14:27 (KJV)

²⁷ "Peace I leave with you, my peace I give unto you: not as the world giveth, give I unto you. Let not your heart be troubled, neither let it be afraid."

God Bless!

NUGGETS TO LIVE BY

SAINTS, YOU ARE NOT ALONE

Saints, Jesus sat with His disciples in the fourteenth chapter of John to comfort them regarding His pending death on the cross. In so doing He shared with them a prayer request that He made on their behalf which says:

John 14:15–16 (KJV)
[15] "If ye love me, keep my commandments. [16] And I will pray the Father, and he shall give you another Comforter, that he may abide with you for ever..."

Saints, those who belong to God demonstrated by their obedience to God, He will not leave us to survive for ourselves alone. Our God loves His children so much that He will not leave us alone as spiritual "orphans"!

🪙 NUGGET ONE

Saints, how many times do your trials seem to get the best of you? How many times does Satan seem to attack you at the most inopportune time? Well, is there an opportune time, really? How many times have you wished Jesus was right there within your eyesight to help you?

Well, Saints, first you are guaranteed that you will be attacked by Satan as children of God. However, praise God, we are not "spiritual orphans"! Why? Because we are God's children and Jesus prayed that we receive another Comforter to come to us when He returned to Heaven. That Comforter will be with you forever, holding your hand all the way to Heaven! Through all your trials and tribulation! All you must do is trust Him! That Comforter is the Holy Spirit!

Ephesians 1:13–14 (KJV)

^{13} "In whom ye also trusted, after that ye heard the Word of truth, the gospel of your salvation: in whom also after that ye believed, ye were sealed with that holy Spirit of promise, ^{14} Which is the earnest of our inheritance until the redemption of the purchased possession, unto the praise of his glory."

NUGGET TWO

Saints, today we as believers were sealed with this Holy Spirit of promised when we gave our lives over to Jesus the Christ!

Friends, why go through this world alone? Believe and trust in our Savior! The Holy Spirit is the promise and pledge from God to them who believe! That you not be alone in this world! Christ is the answer!

Saints, the Holy Spirit is also the guarantee of our inheritance and the first down payment from God. As I always say, "The Holy Spirit will hold your hand all the way to Heaven!" Friends are you ready to have the Holy Spirit guide you through your trials;

to lead you all the way to Heaven to spend an eternity with our God?

Friends I invite you to no longer be strangers and orphans apart from God but to join in with fellow Saints in the household of faith! Are you tired of being tired . . . alone?

Ephesians 2:19–22 (KJV)

[19] "Now therefore ye are no more strangers and foreigners, but fellow citizens with the saints, and of the household of God; [20] And are built upon the foundation of the apostles and prophets, Jesus Christ himself being the chief corner stone; [21] In whom all the building fitly framed together groweth unto an holy temple in the Lord: [22] In whom ye also are builded together for an habitation of God through the Spirit."

God Bless!

NUGGETS TO LIVE BY

SAINTS, BECOMING MORE LIKE JESUS IN OUR PRAISE

Saints, **2 Corinthians 3:18** reminds us that we are continually being transformed as we gaze at the glory of the Lord!

Saints, we are charged to love the unlovable, forgive the unworthy, and to do good to those who cannot reciprocate. However, this charge is impossible in our flesh. We must be transformed! We must be more like Jesus who loved the unlovable, forgave the unworthy, and did good for those who could not reciprocate.

Saints, as we gaze into the glass, we can see the glory of God in each of us. His glory that sustains us and brought us this far! His glory that many times has made a way out of no way! His glory that has given us peace in hectic, trying times because we trusted Him!

Ah, Saints, David realized this in **Psalm 138**. David realized that we are transformed into the image of our Lord through our praise. Let us look at a few Nuggets:

NUGGET ONE

First, David reminds us that to have this transforming praise, we must praise our Lord in the way He desires to be praise.

David says we are to praise the Lord with our "whole heart," with sincerity and personally.

David also reminds us that no other gods will steal his praising to our Lord when he says, "Before other gods he will sing praises." Saints, we see the world today attempting to have gods that steal our praise and singing to our Lord. Sunday, NFL, MLB, Golf, etc. Wednesdays, youth sports practices, etc.

David says He will sing his praises before other gods and he will worship and praise in the temple! Today **Hebrews 10:25** reminds us that we too are to not forsake assembling together the more we see the day approaching of the return of our Lord.

Saints, you want to be transformed; have you gazed in the mirror? How is your praise life? Are you singing God's praises before other worldly gods? Are you a working, praising church member or a country club member?

Let us look at the reasons David is being transformed into the image of the Lord by his praise. David is being transformed from *"glory to glory"*!

NUGGET TWO

David says, ***"Thou hast magnified thy Word above all thy name"***! Saints, David is recognizing our Lord for His faithfulness to him. The Lord promised David He would deliver Him, He would be present with him, and He answers David's prayers!

Ah, Saints, can you also say our Lord has magnified His Word to you? Isn't that worthy of praising Him the way He wants to be praised?

David also continues to speak from his heart when tells our Lord that if the Lord did not deliver him, He did give David strength to make it through! Saints, you have heard some of the elderly say,

"Lord don't move the mountain, just give me the strength to climb!" That is becoming more like Jesus, my friend!

David further praises our Lord when he says, *"Tho I walk in the midst of trouble thou wilt revive me"*! WOW, Saints, David knew that our Lord would make him new! How many times, Saints, has our Lord done that very thing for you? How many times has the Lord made your enemies your footstool and made your crooked road straight, such that you learn to trust Him more and more?

Does your praise life reflect this? For though our Lord be high, he cares for the lowly! Are you being transformed by your praise, Saints?

NUGGET THREE

David ends his psalm by giving all power to our Lord for transforming him into His image:

Psalm 138:8 (KJV)
⁸"The LORD will perfect that which concerneth me: thy mercy, O LORD, endureth for ever: forsake not the works of thine own hands."

Paul in the New Testament confidently puts it this way regarding our Lord's transforming power:

Philippians 1:6 (KJV)
⁶"Being confident of this very thing, that he which hath begun a good work in you will perform it until the day of Jesus Christ."

Saints, He alone is worthy of our praise . . . *AMEN*? Are you being transformed by your praise life?

God Bless!

SAINTS, DO YOU HAVE MORE FAITH IN MAN THAN IN GOD?

Saints, I must assume that one hundred percent of you as redeemed saints would answer this question with a resounding "NO!" So, I have a few questions for you:

How many of you would fly on a commercial flight if you knew that your pilot barely passed his certification to earn his pilot's license?

How many of you would yet fly if you had the opportunity to see the maintenance record of the plane and realize that the records demonstrate a gross negligence of abiding to federal standards?

How many of you would allow a surgeon to perform life-threatening surgery on you if you found he received his degree by having someone else take his tests for him in medical school?

Saints, sadly many Christians do this every day. We board planes having faith in the pilot and the maintenance of the airplane and ride in that faith all the way to our destination. Many Christians also have total faith in their surgeons in life-threatening surgeries and faithfully allow them to put them to sleep and take over their faculties, not to mention after their surgery hanging on every word of the diagnosis!

🪙 NUGGET ONE

Saints, why is it that one can so readily have faith to allow man to take one to their destination through the air or hang on a doctor's every word, when they know so little, if anything about that pilot, that doctor, or their equipment?

More questions, Saints:

When you first accepted Jesus Christ as your Lord and Savior, did you believe that God loved you so much that He sacrificed His Son just for you to be redeemed back to Him?

When you first accepted Christ, did you believe that Christ's death on the cross paid your sin debt forever?

When you first accepted Christ, did you believe that His resurrection confirms that you live because Christ lives and sits at the right hand of God interceding on your behalf?

When you first accepted Christ, did you have faith to believe that He would never leave or forsake you no matter what you are going through?

🪙 NUGGET TWO

Saints, if you are not walking with Christ, whom you should know, to your destination (heaven) in FAITH, but you trust a pilot that you do not know . . . that is putting faith in man more than faith in God!

If you are trusting the plane to take you to your destination through ice, rain, and snow and not trusting the Holy Spirit to take you to heaven through trials, good times and bad, then Saints you are trusting equipment that you do not know versus the Holy Spirit that you should know!

If you are hanging on every word that the surgeon says in a life and death situation, but not hanging on every Word from our Lord in all situations, then you are trusting man who you do not know versus God's Word which you should know!

Saints, we must be careful that when we accept Jesus Christ as our Savior it does not stop there! We must have the same FAITH that brought us to God to serve, trust, love, and obey God in all circumstances good and bad. Trusting and relying on God to bring us back to Him that when we close our eyes here we will open them in Paradise and see Jesus!

Sadly, some Christians expect the long-term change of salvation with a short-term effort of FAITH. Meaning as soon as it gets tough, some Christians' FAITH seem to wane instead of getting stronger as we rely and trust on a mighty God! Remember, Saints, without FAITH it is impossible to please God! **(Heb. 11:6)**

Saints, many Christians have received peace and joy in sustaining the same FAITH we have in our God as when we first came to Him through the blood of Jesus! I leave you with something to think about. In this Scripture, Paul is allowing God to use him to remind the Colossians to do just that:

Colossians 2:6–7 (KJV)
"As ye have therefore received Christ Jesus the Lord,
so walk ye in him: Rooted and built up in him,
and stablished in the faith, as ye have been taught,
abounding therein with thanksgiving."

Ye faithfully received ye ought with that same faith faithfully serve, trust and obey, Saints! Long-term change requires long-term FAITH!

God Bless!

NUGGETS TO LIVE BY

SAINTS, DO YOU REALLY KNOW THE POWER, WILL, AND LOVE OF GOD?

Saints, do you really know the POWER of God? When you pray do you leave all your concerns at our Master's feet or as soon as you say amen you rise to take on the task without Him? Do you really know the POWER of God?

Saints, do you really know the WILL of God specifically for your life? Not just the church, family, or friends, but specifically for you? Have you asked Him to tell you and if so did you just hear, or did you listen?

Saints, do you really understand the LOVE that is revealed in the riches of our inheritance? Or do you live day to day ignoring or taking for granted what Christ has done on the cross specifically for you. that we have an inheritance to be cherished every day?

NUGGET ONE

Well, Saints, Jesus' disciples walked with Jesus for three years and did not comprehend the POWER, WILL, and LOVE of God! In John 14 when Jesus was on the way to the cross to redeem man so that man could go directly to the Father, Thomas asked Jesus to show them where He was going and show them the way. Philip asked Jesus to show them the Father and that would satisfy them. Jesus' answer:

John 14:9 (KJV)
***"Jesus saith unto him,* Have I been so long time with you, and yet hast thou not known me, Philip? he that hath seen me hath seen the Father; and how sayest thou then, Shew us the Father?"**

Jesus had walked with them and they had witnessed many miracles and the love of God. Jesus had often told them that He was sent by the Father and that He and the Father were one. They had witnessed God telling them that Jesus was His Son and that they should listen to Him. Yet they still lacked the comprehension of God's POWER, WILL, and, LOVE! Ah, but Saints, how many Saints today have walked with Jesus for many years and are yet still babes in Christ?

So, Pastor, how does one truly comprehend the POWER, WILL, and LOVE of God? I am so glad you asked!

There was a guy by the name of Saul who had the same problem. He too thought he knew God but lacked this true comprehension. There was another by the name of Peter who also lacked this comprehension of our God.

They both came into the full knowledge of God's POWER, WILL, and LOVE once the Holy Spirit of Wisdom entered their hearts. Paul's prayer for the Ephesian church **(Ephesians 1:17–20)** to receive this same Spirit of Wisdom that they would know the POWER, WILL, and LOVE of God!

NUGGET TWO

So, Saints, when we accepted Jesus Christ we too received the Spirit of Wisdom that sealed us as children of God. So why any of us could be found lacking the knowledge of who God is? The Bible reminds us that we are to always be increasing in the knowledge of God . . . ALWAYS, Saints!

First, we must LISTEN and OBEY the Holy Spirit which dwells within us! We must decrease our desires, lusts, and worldly stubbornness and allow and welcome the Holy Spirit to increase in our lives!

Second, we must be in daily biblical study at home and collectively in the church with fellow brothers and sisters in Christ. The Holy Spirit dwells within us to remind us and to teach us what God has for us in His Word. Saints, how many of you know you cannot draw water from an empty well? How many Saints you know are "empty wells" going to church but leaving their Bibles closed the rest of the week? Not going to Bible study, praying, or reading God's Word? How then would they know the POWER, WILL, and LOVE of God? They can't!!

Third, we must cherish our inheritance! That inheritance is that we are "Heaven bound Saints" because of the love of God and the obedience of His Son, Jesus Christ! Saints, focusing on that alone should stimulate our hearts to want to develop a continuous relationship with our loving Father! That should stimulate zeal in us to becoming more acquainted with God daily in study, trusting in prayer, listening and obeying the Holy Spirit which He sent to hold our hands all the way to Heaven!

Finally, Saints, it should also give us a desire to know what God's will is specifically for us to do while we are in this world today . . . and do it!

Saints, when you get to Heaven, will someone have to take you around and introduce you to God? Or will you know Him before you get there?

God Bless!

SAINTS, RELY ON THE STRONG FOR STRENGTH
Psalm 121

Saints, do you ever reach a point where it feels like the world is on top of you? That the world's weight seems to just drain all your energy and strength? That whatever dilemma you may be going through seems to take all your attention and consumes one hundred percent of your focus while with friends, at work, or even while worshipping our God? Many of us have at some time in our past been at this very junction in our Christian walk!

I am using past tense while this may be present tense with some of you right now. If neither, it most assuredly will be future tense. So how does one make this a time of victory versus despair?

NUGGET ONE

Saints, we must rely on the strong for our strength! Our strong God sits high and looks low. Ready to help His children in times of need! Satan desires to keep God's Saints focused on the weight of the world on our backs not just to discourage us but to take this time to divert our focus from the Lord! Satan knows that there is power in the Lord! As long as he is diverting you from our

Lord, he believes you to be vulnerable and defeated and certainly discouraged! David says:

"I will lift up mine eyes unto the hills, from whence cometh my help. My help cometh from the Lord, which made heaven and earth."

Saints, in these times we are to have confidence and patience! Looking to the hills with anticipation of the coming of our Lord to deliver us! If God is powerful enough to create Heaven and Earth, certainly He has power to deliver us as He has promised in His Word. **Saints, look up!** For the power to deliver and the power to sustain you! Our power and strength come from the Lord!

Staying focused on the weight of the world on our backs can cause us to go down a slippery slope of defeat! Making decisions that we otherwise would not apart from relying and waiting on the Lord. David reminds us that our God will not allow our foot to slip in these situations if we would only trust and lean on Him and not on ourselves, Saints! God our strength will not only guide us, but David is reminding us that He will sustain us as well! Guiding our every footstep if only we would listen, Saints!

NUGGET TWO

Saints, He further says that our Lord never naps or sleeps. Imagine while you are finally resting in the peace of the Lord trusting Him, He is still at work in your life and dilemma. That kind of strength, commitment, and love only comes from the Lord! Keeping and preserving His Saints from the burning heat! God is "the shade upon thy right hand." Saints, this is also a picture of our Lord protecting us from the heat of our dilemma as He also fights our battles! The "right hand" was the hand used in battle and carried the sword. David is reminding us to embrace our Lord as our "keeper" and "shade" and the Lord will fight our battles! Fighting them both day and night!

"The Lord is thy keeper: the Lord is thy shade upon thy right hand. The sun shall not smite thee by day, nor the moon by night."

Relying on the strong for our strength!

Saints, only our Lord can protect us with such power. Therefore, David says in other Psalms that God is his "shelter and his strength" and a present help in times of need.

NUGGET THREE

Saints, there was another time that David remained focused on our Lord! That time was when all the army of God was fearful of a man named Goliath. They were focused on their calamity rather than trusting in God. How many of you are focused on your Goliath and not the hills were your strength comes from?

David was so focused that he refused armor and only chose five stones and his slingshot. I believe that David selected five because he was prepared to follow God if he had to use all five!

However, all praises to God as He was not slothful and was on time as God directed the first stone and it hit its mark and Goliath fell! Saints, our Lord can defeat the Goliaths of our lives if only our focus remains on Him! Relying on the strong for our strength! No matter how long we must wait but wait with confidence and assurance of His desire to deliver us His children!

NUGGET FOUR

Saints, what an awesome additional promise to preserve our very soul. If our soul is preserved all is preserved. Imagine the promise of preserving an egg yolk. In order to preserve the yoke, the shell and egg white must be preserved as well. Saints, to preserve our soul is to preserve all of who we are in Christ!

Protecting the most fragile Saint (shell) and heart (egg whites) to preserve our very soul (egg yolk) from evil! Promising as we go out in the morning and come home in the evening we are protected. Or as we come into the world as a child until we go home to glory as an adult we are protected!

Saints, is there any reason, ***any reason at all*** that we can't say too in times of trouble, "I will lift up mine eyes unto the hills, from whence cometh my help"?

I leave you with this Scripture from **Philippians 4:6–7:**
"Be careful for nothing; but in every thing by prayer and supplication with thanksgiving let your requests be made known unto God. And the peace of God, which passeth all understanding, shall keep your hearts and minds through Christ Jesus."

God Bless!

SAINTS, STIR THE KOOL-AID!

Saints, we have learned in our daily walk that it is imperative to trust in our God. We learn through His Word and through the experience of trials that trusting in our Lord is the only way for peace, joy, and victory in this world!

However, Saints, are you aware that our Lord trusts YOU as well? Our Lord trusts each believer with an awesome gift! This gift is so significant that it will supply all that you will ever need to accomplish the mighty task that the Lord is entrusting YOU to accomplish.

This gift is so enabling that it is guaranteed to have success without fail and EVERY ONE OF YOU has it as a believer! The question is do YOU know that our Lord trusts YOU and are YOU living up to that trust?

NUGGET ONE

Saints, **Romans 12** reminds us that our Lord provides a measure of faith to every believer:

Romans 12:3 (KJV)

³"For I say, through the grace given unto me, to every

man that is among you, not to think of himself more highly than he ought to think; but to think soberly, according as God hath dealt to every man the measure of faith."

A measure of faith given to every believer to be receptive to the grace given to each of us to accomplish the task God has specifically assigned to us! That task could be teaching, preaching, pastoring, healing, evangelism, serving, etc.

Saints, let's look at making a pitcher of Kool-Aid. When we add a pack of Kool-Aid to a pitcher of water, it usually settles at the bottom of the pitcher of water with the sugar you have added.

Imagine this Kool-Aid and sugar representing the measure of faith our Lord has given you to do a task that He has trusted only YOU to do but instead of doing that task that you have been entrusted and enabled to do by your gift of you own measure of faith, you do nothing! It is like Kool-Aid and sugar sitting at the bottom of the pitcher!

This Kool-Aid tastes horrible because it has not been stirred! Well, Saints, there are many "pew riders" and Saints that have been enabled to accomplish a God-given task with their very own measure of faith and it has simply settled in their hearts, unstirred and creating only a "tasteless," powerless Christian.

NUGGET TWO

Saints, have you taken the time to go to our Lord and ask Him what it is that He wants to entrust you to do? Not you church, pastor, or deacon but YOU, specifically? You have the enabling already sitting there in you waiting to be stirred! Are you a Saint on

Sunday, but a tasteless, powerless Christian the other six days? If so, you are without excuse!

Yes, as I stated earlier, we trust God as we walk with Him, but can God say that He can trust you with what He has given to you? Can God even say that you have even asked Him what it is?

My friends, this world is dark with sin and disdain for our God and it is getting darker every day, but I believe this is also a testimony of Christians' lack of "Stirring the Kool-Aid"! Stirring the measure of faith entrusted in every believer to make an impact in this world that would shake Satan himself and cause him to run!

Saints, Paul took his measure of faith and allowed God to stir it within him and completed the task entrusted to him. Can you say the same?

Saints, it is time to "STIR THE KOOL-AID"!

1 Timothy 1:13–14 (KJV)

[13] "Who was before a blasphemer, and a persecutor, and injurious: but I obtained mercy, because I did it ignorantly in unbelief. [14] And the grace of our Lord was exceeding abundant with faith and love which is in Christ Jesus."

God Bless!

NUGGETS TO LIVE BY

SAINTS, WE HAVE OUR MARCHING ORDERS
John 15:1–8

Years ago as a youngster, I would watch the television show called *Mission Impossible* with my family. I am now reminded of the beginning when the agents would receive their orders. Their orders seemed utterly impossible! Then the narrator would always say "This is your mission, if you choose to accept it." They never rejected a mission, no matter the difficulty!

Saints, in this portion of Scripture we too have been given our mission! The question is, have you accepted it?

In our text, Jesus has given the mission for us to bear much fruit. That mission may seem to be impossible, but he prefaced it by alerting us that He is the "True Vine." Also, that we are the "branches."

When looking at this descriptive imaging, one must take note of the significance of the vine Jesus is referencing. A vine is very vital to the growth of the branches, as it provides strength and nourishment needed by the branches. This alone is vital to the branches being able to live and provide much fruit.

🏷 NUGGET ONE

Saints, many vineyards even today sell vines to other vineyards at a premium cost, primarily because vines are significant to the success of the branches to bear much fruit for the success of their business. The vine's only purpose is to strengthen the branches to produce. The branch's responsibility is to produce the fruit by the strength of the vine that is only committed to them and the fruit. Hence **Philippians 4:13** where Paul says, *"I can do all things through Christ which strengtheneth me."*

The danger is the strength, nourishment, and protection lost by the branch being detached from this valuable life source the "True Vine." This very vine that only has the branch's interest at heart! Jesus warning that detachment from Him will result in being withered and being cast into the fire.

It is important to recognize that while this is referring to the fire of hell as mentioned in **Revelation 20:15** and **21:8**, it is also speaking of the present time.

🏷 NUGGET TWO

Saints, this is also referring to our current fiery trials and temptations that we will face without the strength needed for spiritual battle that can only come from the "True Vine"! We must remain connected to this valuable vine as our source of victory for pending trials and temptations. If you find yourselves empty of strength in your trials and temptations, the question is, are you connected to the "True Vine"? In His Word, studying, meditating, and praying?

We have an awesome promise in verse 7! God says that *"if ye abide in me, and **my word** abide in you..."* True harmony with Christ to remain connected to the True Vine is allowing God's Word to richly dwell within the believer. It is like "Miracle Gro" for the branches!

God's Word dwelling in us, controlling our very thoughts, our will, and actions keeps us in harmony with Christ. Hence, our will is no longer in charge and we now are filled with Christ's will that is in harmony with Him, and now we have confidence that our prayer life is heard and will receive the best possible answer. No matter what that answer is . . .

1 John 5:14–15
"And this is the confidence that we have in him, that, if we ask any thing according to his will, he heareth us: And if we know that he hear us, whatsoever we ask, we know that we have the petitions that we desired of him."

Saints, what an awesome promise to have our prayers heard! Allow our Savior's will to overtake our will as we remain in harmony with Christ!

While our text is referring to winning souls, it is describing much more. There are initially three different types of fruit that the text is referring to. Two of them must be fruitful before even beginning to win souls.

The first is recognizing that Christ nourishes believers to be abundantly fruitful in CHARACTER! The character that glorifies our Father, God! The character that reveals to all that we serve the Lord! The character that keeps us together as believers! That character is referred to as the Fruit of The Spirit, found in **Galatians 5:22–23**!

"But the fruit of the Spirit is love, joy, peace, longsuffering, gentleness, goodness, faith, meekness, temperance: against such there is no law."

The second is recognizing that Christ nourishes believers to be abundantly fruitful in EVERY GOOD WORK! Allowing God to sanctify us by molding us to His will in all our works! This can only be done if we succumb to His will in everything. Hence, giving in to His will in our actions demonstrates to the world how close we are to our heavenly Father as we learn more of Him and His intentions for our life. We can only do this by the strength of the "True Vine"! **Colossians 1:10** says,

"That ye might walk worthy of the Lord unto all pleasing, being fruitful in every good work, and increasing in the knowledge of God . . ."

NUGGET THREE

Saints, how can we win souls apart from the "True Vine," Jesus Christ? Secondly, how can we win souls without a godly, fruitful character and fruitful, godly works? If our character and actions are the same as the world, who can we win? No one!

The greatest confirmation of our attachment to the "True Vine" is when the world sees Christ in us! And this is enhanced when one asks you what they must do to be saved. This can only be done through Jesus Christ nourishing us as believers. We cannot do this on our own!

Now we are ready to finish our mission should we choose to accept it! That is winning souls for our Savior! Accomplishing this by glorifying Him who has strengthened us to accomplish this mission! He has not only given strength but has equipped us as well. Finally, he will be with us throughout the mission as we stay attached to Him, the "True Vine":

"Go ye therefore, and teach all nations, baptizing them in the name of the Father, and of the Son, and of the Holy Ghost: Teaching them to observe all things whatsoever I have commanded you: and, lo, I am with you always, even unto the end of the world. Amen." (Matt. 28:19–20)

God Bless!

NUGGETS TO LIVE BY

SAINTS, WE HAVE THE BEST BENEFITS PACKAGE

Saints, we recently embarked on an ugly part of our history here in America. We witnessed the campaigning for various offices of our government, including the office of the President of the United States.

The mudslinging lies and accusations ran rampant and without shame! Friends and neighbors found themselves at odds with one another! I wonder how many countries watched this spectacle and shook their heads in bewilderment? I believe God Himself was not pleased with most of what happened.

One side claims that they are Christians and will not demonstrate Christian values in loving their brothers, taking care of the poor, and fairness in their wealth and responsibility to others. The other side ignores many Christian values and tries to demonstrate that God's Word is outdated and unrealistic. Both challenge Christians to stand up for Christian values and condemn those who do not as not Christians!

NUGGET ONE

Saints, more than ever we must realize that as Christians we have the best benefits package of all time and that package is better than the one offered by this world! This world will try to tell us as believers that we are weak, that we are behind the times. That man knows what we need.

Saints, this year I am going to put a sign in my yard that says, *"VOTE JESUS FOR THE BEST BENEFITS A MAN CAN HOPE FOR—JOHN 3:16!"*

Saints, these benefits will never be repealed, ridiculed by the giver, or used to promote wars for financial gain for a select few. These benefits will be between our God and His people. Not subject to the whims of a high court because a much Higher Court has established them!

The best benefit we have is to be called the sons (and daughters) of God!

John 1:11–12 (KJV)

"He came unto his own, and his own received him not. But as many as received him, to them gave he power to become the sons of God, even to them that believe on his name."

NUGGET TWO

Saints, no matter what the world offers or the "candidates" offer, they cannot offer a better benefit package than one offered by our God through the blood of our Savior Jesus Christ! Our God even sealed it with the best down payment, The Holy Spirit:

Ephesians 1:13–14 (KJV)

"In whom ye also trusted, after that ye heard the Word of truth, the gospel of your salvation: in whom also after that ye believed, ye were sealed with that holy Spirit of promise, which is the earnest of our inheritance until the

redemption of the purchased possession, unto the praise of his glory."

Saints, both sides will try to deceive us as Christians. That should not surprise us because of Satan, the prince of this world!

However, all praises to our Heavenly Father because the last page of our benefits package guarantees our ultimate home will be with Him! The assurance is the Holy Spirit which will hold our hands all the way through this life, all the way to Heaven, by guiding, teaching, and reminding us of the Word of God, Himself!

Therefore, Saints, refuse to be lead away from God's Word to man's word. Keep your hands in the one who has made the best unchangeable, guaranteed benefits package and signed it in His Son's blood, our Father God!

Hebrews 13:14–15 (KJV)
"For here have we no continuing city, but we seek one to come. By him therefore let us offer the sacrifice of praise to God continually, that is, the fruit of our lips giving thanks to his name."

God Bless!

NUGGETS TO LIVE BY

SAINTS, WHO KNOWS AND LOVES YOU BEST?

Saints, I have asked this question many times to many different people, only to receive some very surprising answers. Answers ranging from their mom, father, wife, pastor or sibling.

Saints, one only must go to God's Word to realize the true answer!

I am particularly drawn to one of David's Psalms. In this Psalm, David has twenty-two verses of which three verses answer the question of who knows us best and the remainder answer the question of who loves us best. That Psalm is 103!

NUGGET ONE

In verses 14–16, God's Word reminds us that God knows how we were formed. That we were formed by Him from mere dust and He breathed life in us and we became a living soul.

As dust we are without strength, weak, and unstable! Saints, God knows best all our weaknesses and instabilities for He formed us.

God also knows that the winds of time will further weaken us with trials and tribulations that impact our lives as we age day by day. For we are like a flower that withers in time and gone and forgotten.

Saints, who best to love you than one who knows you best?

NUGGET TWO

The remaining nineteen verses, God expresses the love He has for us as His children. Nuggets such as His ability and desire to forgive our weaknesses and instabilities. What an awesome God we serve, Saints! On this side of the cross, we realize His forgiving power through His only begotten Son Jesus! That while we were yet sinners, He sent His Son to redeem us! No greater love than when one lays down His life for His brother!

NUGGET THREE

God loves us so much that he also promises to heal and deliver us from destruction. Saints, we dare call on man for deliverance as we realize man is either powerless or lacks desire to deliver. Our God desires, promises, and has the ultimate power to deliver His children from destruction. He alone stands ready to answer our call. After all, we are His "miracle children."

NUGGET FOUR

Saints, man is quick to anger and hold grudges, but in this Psalm, David points out that our God is slow to anger and does not hold grudges. While being full of mercy and pity! WOW! Who would know that better than David?

Saints, we all have at some point realized the wrath of God as He has justly punished us for our sins, but we know that in His punishment, He is just and patient with us! We also know that when He forgives, it is done never to be brought up again! Praises be to God for such awesome love!

The mercy of the Lord is from everlasting to everlasting; praise His Holy Name, Saints! He alone knows us best and He alone loves us most... bless His Holy Name!

David so fittingly ends this Psalm like this:

Psalm 103:21–22 (AMP)
[21] "Bless (affectionately, gratefully praise) the Lord, all you His hosts, you His ministers who do His pleasure. [22] Bless the Lord, all His works in all places of His dominion; bless (affectionately, gratefully praise) the Lord, O my soul!"

God Bless!

NUGGETS TO LIVE BY

SATAN CAN HURT A WELL-DRESSED SOLDIER

Saints, without one ingredient, Satan will hurt a well-dressed soldier. From start to finish, a salty warrior for Christ seeking his crown is in a war! Praise God we are given our uniform in Ephesians.

God's Word instructs us to:
- Stand and have our loins girt about with truth
- Have on the breastplate of righteousness
- Our feet shod with the preparation of the gospel of peace
- Taking the shield of faith
- Taking the helmet of salvation
- Taking the sword of the Spirit

Now Saints, that is a well-dressed, salty warrior for Christ! Many times we see this preached and taught in our churches absent from the remaining ingredient that will ensure ourselves from being hurt by Satan.

NUGGET ONE

Saints, God's Word gives the crucial ingredient right after the dress requirement:

Ephesians 6:18 (KJV)
¹⁸ "Praying always with all prayer and supplication in the Spirit, and watching thereunto with all perseverance and supplication for all saints . . ."

Saints, it is imperative that a salty warrior for our Lord maintain a healthy prayer life! In other words, making sure that he or she remains connected to God as we fight this war on Earth! A vigorous prayer life is a constant fellowship with our Lord!

Just as nowhere in the text does it say to remove the armor, we should never lose our fellowship through prayer with our Lord. Doing so would put us at risk of being vulnerable to Satan's schemes.

NUGGET TWO

A salty warrior should pray while marching and while fighting! Praying in good times and in bad times! Many times, as a warrior, one may forget to pray when things are going well, or pray less fervently than one would if things were going bad.

God's Word is clear, we are to be both fervently thankful and sorrowful in prayer as we remain vigilant.

NUGGET THREE

Saints, a salty warrior is instructed to "pray in the Spirit." Salty warriors are to not pray self-willed, shallow prayers but only in God's will. That is why we pray by the direction of the Holy Spirit that dwells within the salty warrior!

The Holy Spirit will only direct God's warrior to pray fervently to God, no one else!

> **Romans 8:26–27 (KJV)**
> *²⁶ "Likewise, the Spirit also helpeth our infirmities: for we know not what we should pray for as we ought: but the Spirit itself maketh intercession for us with groanings which cannot be uttered. ²⁷ And he that searcheth the hearts knoweth what is the mind of the Spirit, because he maketh intercession for the saints according to the will of God."*

In our prayer life, remember our God is a jealous God and He sent Jesus Christ to make a way for us to go directly to His throne in prayer. As long as we come in the Spirit in Jesus' name, Saints!

NUGGET FOUR

Saints, we must be intensely involved in prayer! Have you ever stayed awake at night in prayer? Have you ever lost track of time in prayer? Has God ever stopped you in prayer to talk to you and it was like drinking water from a fire hose?

Jesus admonished His disciples for not staying awake while praying! Saints, the battle is an ongoing battle and Satan is working overtime seeking to destroy you! We must persevere in our prayer life! A salty warrior does not quickly bless his food and quickly say only morning and evening prayers! Need I say more?

Finally, we must always pray for our brothers and sisters in this battle. Fervently seeking God's will, direction, health, and strength for those who share in this battle. Calling each by name whenever possible.

Our prayer for them should be as intense as our prayers are for ourselves, for we are not on this battlefield alone . . .

God Bless!

NUGGETS TO LIVE BY

SATAN, YOU BETTER HELP THE BEAR!

Saints, my aunt, when confronted by difficulties or rivalries, would always say, "If you see me and a bear fighting, you better help the bear!" What an awesome attitude! She made one believe that she had some sort of an awesome power inside her that assured victory over whatever was before her! She made us believe that no matter the pending struggle, she was prepared to make it and succeed!

Saints, this is how we should live our spiritual lives as we face trials along this Christian journey in a place we call Earth!

NUGGET ONE
Philippians 4:13 (KJV)
"I can do all things through Christ which strengtheneth me."

Saints, we should have every confidence that no matter what trial we are facing, our God will provide us the strength to make it through. Our faith should say "Amen" to our Father's "I got this!" We, like my aunt, should say to Satan, "You better help the bear!"

We too ought to be prepared to go through the battle with our confidence of faith in our God!

In **1 Samuel 17** David was watching the sheep and in came a lion and a bear and took a defenseless little lamb out of the flock. The Scripture said that David went out to get the lamb!

NUGGET TWO

Saints, nowhere in the text did it say that David waited, cried, or delayed his response to this trial! Nor does it say that David was afraid!

Saints, he immediately responded to the trial head on! How many times do we out of fear allow our trials to take the best of us rather than see God's strength in our trials? Strength enough to attack the bear and lion of our trials head on and tell Satan he better help them because I got God on my side! Our prayer should be that God will reveal Himself to us in our trials in that we do not see the trial but God's victory in the trial! Saints, David saw the power of God in his trial of saving a little defenseless lamb. As a result, David killed both the lion and the bear! That demonstration of active faith, Saints, pleases our God. Before you attack the lion and bear of your trial, do you see the power of God driving your faith?

Hebrews 11:6 (KJV)
"But without faith it is impossible to please him: for he that cometh to God must believe that he is, and that he is a rewarder of them that diligently seek him."

Saints, David did something that is notable before he was confronted by this trial. He was watching the sheep!

NUGGET THREE

Saints, David was doing the work of the Lord. He had been called to watch the sheep. David was not slack in doing God's work no matter the challenge of weather, terrain, night, or day. Saints, when confronted by your trials, do they find you doing God's work? Are you being watchful and steadfast in the faith?

Saints, our bold, courageous spirit does not start *IN* our trials, it starts as we walk with the Lord obeying and doing His will! Many times, the cause of weak faith in our trials is the lack of faith exercised outside of our trials. How can one demonstrate courageous faith during a trial when one fails to demonstrate it in obedience and trusting our Father's guidance for our lives, outside of our trials?

Saints, if you want to tell Satan, if he sees you fighting the bears of your trials that he needs to help the bear, then you better know Jesus!

Paul gave this message to the Philippians and I leave it for you, Saints:

Philippians 1:27–28 (KJV)

"Only let your conversation be as it becometh the gospel of Christ: that whether I come and see you, or else be absent, I may hear of your affairs, that ye stand fast in one spirit, with one mind striving together for the faith of the gospel;
And in nothing terrified by your adversaries: which is to them an evident token of perdition, but to you of salvation, and that of God."

God Bless!

NUGGETS TO LIVE BY

SNATCHING VICTORY FROM THE JAWS OF DEFEAT

Saints, the devil is certainly on the loose! How many of you know that this world is trying to have victory over the children of God?

The world with its trials and temptations consistently attempts to hinder the children of God from obeying our Father's Word! All the while telling God's children that God's Word is too atrocious to follow. The world telling God's children that God's Word is "subject to interpretation."

Recently there were two Supreme Court decisions that propelled this nation into bedlam! The decision on legalizing "same sex marriage" for all fifty States brought both roaring disagreement and roaring applause. The world's acceptance of what God clearly calls an abomination and promised judgment needs no interpretation but obedience!

My son Nick puts it this way, *"Why is this country in such a hurry to meet the fate of Sodom and Gomorrah?"*

Another Supreme Court decision that incensed this country was the Affordable Care Act or what has been named Obamacare. God's Word is clear that we should open our hands wide to those that are poor and in need. Yet many are yet incensed by the Supreme Court decision, when it clearly meets God's Word:

Deuteronomy 15:7–11 (KJV)

"If there be among you a poor man of one of thy brethren within any of thy gates in thy land which the LORD thy God giveth thee, thou shalt not harden thine heart, nor shut thine hand from thy poor brother: [8] But thou shalt open thine hand wide unto him, and shalt surely lend him sufficient for his need, in that which he wanteth. Beware that there be not a thought in thy wicked heart, saying, The seventh year, the year of release, is at hand; and thine eye be evil against thy poor brother, and thou givest him nought; and he cry unto the LORD against thee, and it be sin unto thee. Thou shalt surely give him, and thine heart shall not be grieved when thou givest unto him: because that for this thing the LORD thy God shall bless thee in all thy works, and in all that thou puttest thine hand unto. For the poor shall never cease out of the land: therefore I command thee, saying, Thou shalt open thine hand wide unto thy brother, to thy poor, and to thy needy, in thy land."

NUGGET ONE

Saints, so how in a world that does not know God nor has the Spirit of God can a child of God avoid being defeated? Saints, **1 John 5:1–5** gives us three points to having victory by being snatched out of this world's jaws of defeat!

FIRST: We must trust and rely on the fact that Jesus Christ is The Christ. That he came to give life and to give it more abundantly! Also, that as the special, unique one of the Father, He alone we must trust and rely on! In so doing we rely and follow His Word that was given to Him by the Father for us and left in His Bible for us to follow and obey, not question, add to, or interpret to meet our fleshly needs, but to glorify God!

Helping the poor glorifies God! Fulfilling man's lusts in homosexuality glorifies man and not God! As Rome and Sodom realized in their judgment, so too will the United States also be judged.

Second: Our 1 John 5 text reminds us that those who are born of God and love God will keep His commandments and they are not grievous.

NUGGET TWO

Saints, God's commandments will not be grievous for a born-again Christian because he has died to self and risen unto new life—reborn! Now as a new creature in Christ, our will is lost inside His will and we see the world through Christ not our flesh:

> **Galatians 2:20 (KJV)**
> *"I am crucified with Christ: nevertheless I live; yet not I, but Christ liveth in me: and the life which I now live in the flesh I live by the faith of the Son of God, who loved me, and gave himself for me."*

Saints, as born-again Christians, we have the very nature of God in us, **2 Peter 1:3–4**. We also have everything pertaining to life and godliness. Hence, following God and His commandments are not atrocious to follow for a born-again Christian, but life!

THIRD: We must as born-again believers stay bound together. What better way to be bound together than our love for one another! Love is the greatest bond we as children of God can have to escape the jaws of defeat in this world.

Satan will continue to darken this world if the "sons of God" remain divided and dormant! Specifically, those who remain quiet about this world's abominations such as homosexuality, assuming God is pleased and will handle it when He has called us to speak up about it, warning those who are slaves to its sin!

NUGGET THREE

Saints, God desires that we as born-again Christians obey God's Holy Word, love one another as He loves us! After all we have the same God, same Father, same rebirth, same divine nature, and same adoption! Therefore, we must remain united in a fervent love of fellow Christians, doing the work we have been subpoenaed to do! That work is spreading God's Word in our walk, talk, and demeanor. Letting the world know when it is wrong and against God's Holy Word. Homosexuality and closing our hands to the poor is not only wrong but it is against God's Holy Word . . . ***PERIOD!***

1 Peter 1:22–23 (KJV)

"Seeing ye have purified your souls in obeying the truth through the Spirit unto unfeigned love of the brethren, see that ye love one another with a pure heart fervently: Being born again, not of corruptible seed, but

of incorruptible, by the Word of God, which liveth and abideth for ever."

God Bless!

NUGGETS TO LIVE BY

STAYING IN THE CENTER OF THE ROAD
Proverbs 4:26−27 (KJV)

> ²⁶ *"Ponder the path of thy feet, and let all thy ways be established.*
> ²⁷ *Turn not to the right hand nor to the left: remove thy foot from evil."*

Saints, every morning I attempt to prepare a "DO" list of things that need to be accomplished that day and throughout the week. Many of you probably do the same.

The goal also is to prevent me from being sidetracked and to help me stay focus on getting things done. Despite all my efforts, there are always obstacles throughout the day or week that cause potential chaos to my plans.

NUGGET ONE

Proverbs is reminding us that we are to first "PONDER" the path God has for us each day. Before we take the first step each day we are to make a straight and level path for our feet to travel. A spiritual "DO" list!

Saints, we do this as God's children by staying focused on this God-given path by keeping our eyes forward because if we look right or left, we could stumble!

Saints, I love the game of chess. Online, I play daily various people across the world. Many times I find myself playing as many as five to six people at once! Of course, there is no time limit between moves. However, before I send my move to my opponent, I see the move first and attempt to see what options this move leaves for my rival.

NUGGET TWO

Proverbs is warning us to do the same thing in our Spiritual lives daily. Before we get out of bed we are to ponder or weigh our actions for the day before we act. Will our plans that day glorify God or glorify ourselves?

Will our plans and actions put us on our knees before God's throne in shame or in gratitude this day of the path traveled?

That is why the Proverb says, *"Let all thy ways be established."* Saints, we must look at the blueprint of our actions before we do them daily. We have a Christian obligation to verify that the actions we plan to take each day are ordered by God Himself.

One does this by lining up our planned actions with God's Word. If it is not in God's Word, it is NOT a course of action to consider at all! Only those daily actions prescribed by the Word of God are to be considered!

NUGGET THREE

Saints, Proverbs also says we are to let those ways be established—meaning that we are to be prepared to stand firm in them as we move down the very center of the road that day. We do this with the utmost Spiritual confidence because we are now assured that it is God ordering our steps and not "yours truly"!

Saints, what is your path today? Have you pondered and confirmed it by God's Word? Are you prepared to stand firm and stay in the center, avoiding looking to the right or left? If your answer is no, get with our Father before starting your day! If your answer is yes, have a blessed, marvelous day:

> **Psalm 119:132–133 (KJV)**
> [132] *"Look thou upon me, and be merciful unto me, as thou usest to do unto those that love thy name.* [133] *Order my steps in thy Word: and let not any iniquity have dominion over me."*

God Bless!

NUGGETS TO LIVE BY

TAKING GOD'S KINDNESS FOR WEAKNESS
1 Corinthians 6:9-11

Saints, this may not be one of those "feel good" nuggets, as it deals with a subject that is most avoided by many pulpits across this nation. That subject is sin and its detrimental effect on all who dwell in it!

My favorite R&B singer in college was Isaac Hayes, who sang a song with the lyrics that said he was being taken advantage of by someone taking his kindness for weakness.

Many of us have experienced God as a healer, a peacemaker, a counselor, a provider, and a deliverer. Also, one who fights our battles and protects us at every turn. As well as our strength in time of need!

Still, many know the anguish and pain Jesus experienced on the cross for our sins and yet continue to dwell in sin taking God's grace and kindness for weakness!

NUGGET ONE

Saints, did you know that Jesus came to bring fire upon the earth and that He wished that it was already kindled! (Look at

Luke 12:49–50) Yes, Jesus came to bring peace on earth, but he also came to bring "fire"!

That fire is referencing the fact that Jesus was sent by God to bring judgment. Demonstrating the judgment of death on the cross for sin. The text further says that Jesus was to be baptized with the judgment of death for our sins. Pressured to get the salvation plan completed on the cross for you and for me!

When one ponders the awesome grace and kindness that was done on the cross for you and I, how could one continue to dwell in sin and take God's grace and kindness for weakness?

Romans 2:1–5

This passage is a warning to those who judge and dwell in sin themselves. In verse 4 it teaches much more. That those who do not take the "riches of God's goodness" and let it lead them to repentance would face the righteous judgment of God! Righteous in that God sees the inner man and knows his heart. Therefore, as one writer puts it, God will judge the truth, the whole truth, and nothing but the truth! Those who dwell in sin cannot hide anything from Him!

NUGGET TWO

Saints, we must be careful not to dwell in sin! Not to take the "Riches of God's goodness" for weakness!

Some believe that their own "goodness" is too good for God to punish them. They believe that they can compel God to overlook their punishment. After all, God is too kind and full of grace!

Saints, when we embrace God's kindness and grace, we have a choice to allow it to bring us to our knees for sin or despise it by ignoring it and taking it for weakness in God!

Yet others may believe that they are good enough to enter the Kingdom based on what they do or think. They may do "good works" or have "good tendencies." They may attend church regularly and work in various ministries, yet offering this as a payment of dwelling in sin!

My friends, the Bible says that a man's own righteousness is like "filthy rags"!

NUGGET THREE

Saints, God demands perfection! Man is not perfect; hence, man is not acceptable to God! That is why man must repent and turn to God for God's righteousness and perfection. Man, simply cannot do this for himself!

So how does the imperfect man do this? Glad you asked! By giving his life to Christ! Then allowing God to sanctify him and prepare him for the return of Jesus Christ:

Philippians 1:6
Paul says, *"Being confident of this very thing that He which hath begun a good work in you will perform it until the day of Jesus Christ."*

We must allow God to do His work within us and clean us up. We do this by listening, obeying, and following Him as we hold the Holy Spirit's hand all the way to Heaven, Saints!

Finally, there are still those who feel they can escape the punishment of sin altogether. That our God is weak and can be "snowed." Maybe God has too much on His plate to know or realize the sin one may be sold out to. Sadly, there are many professed believers that feel this way.

Luke 12:2 says, *"For there is nothing covered, that shall not be revealed, neither hid, that shall not be known."*

No one will be able to hide—not believers, professed believers, nor those who take God's kindness for weakness!

NUGGET FOUR

In **Matthew 25:31–33, 41** God's Word says, that on that day he will separate the sheep from the goats. Which will you be? **1 Corinthians 6:9–11** lists the sins that will not allow one to enter the Kingdom! Any of them you are dwelling in?

It also says that we all were once in them, but true believers have been washed . . . no longer to dwell in them again!

I leave you with David's prayer that we as true believers should adopt in our daily prayer life:

Psalm 139:23–24

"Search me, O God, and know my heart: try me, and know my thoughts: and see if there be any wicked way in me, and lead me in the way everlasting."

God Bless!

THE IMAGE OF A CHRISTIAN

Saints, historically believers and governments have jostled for control over one another. In times past the early church fighting to make government subject to the church and the government fighting to make the early church subject to the government.

We see this even today as believers continue to attempt to make the government subject to them with such Supreme Court battles as done by Hobby Lobby—which by the way is a slippery slope that will come back to haunt this country.

We also see our government continue to fight to make believers subject to the government with such decisions as same-sex marriage, eliminating prayer and bibles out of our public schools and the like. By the way these decisions too are a slippery slope which continues to be detrimental to our society.

So, what is a believer to do, Saints?

NUGGET ONE

In Scripture God has given us this commandment. Paul told Titus in **Titus 3:1**:

Titus 3:1 (KJV)
"Put them in mind to be subject to principalities and powers, to obey magistrates, to be ready to every good work..."

Peter told the Jews that had been robbed of their wealth and exiled from their land by the pagan King Nero:

1 Peter 2:13–16 (KJV)
"Submit yourselves to every ordinance of man for the Lord's sake: whether it be to the king, as supreme; Or unto governors, as unto them that are sent by him for the punishment of evildoers, and for the praise of them that do well. For so is the will of God, that with well doing ye may put to silence the ignorance of foolish men: As free, and not using your liberty for a cloke of maliciousness, but as the servants of God."

These were instructions given to believers while under pagan governments! Yes, we are to obey God rather than man when laws clash against God's law. We must be careful to do this to the glory of God in a spirit of winning souls for the kingdom. To quote verse 16, **"As free, and not using your liberty for a cloke of maliciousness, but as the servants of God."**

Jesus gave this example when he was approached by those Jews who were attempting to trick Him regarding paying taxes to Caesar in **Luke 20:20–26**. Jesus gave an answer that marveled them and is good for us even today as we function in a pagan government. He pointed out the "image" on the coin and said:

Luke 20:25–26 (KJV)

*"And he said unto them, **render therefore unto Caesar the things which be Caesar's, and unto God the things which be God's.** And they could not take hold of his words before the people: and they marveled at his answer, and held their peace."*

NUGGET TWO

Saints, as we walk this Christian journey, we must remember that we are the very "image" of Christ under what can be called a pagan government (Democrat & Republican). That image was bestowed on us by God when we accepted His son. That image becomes clearer as we grow closer to God in obedience, prayer, trials, study, and worship. Scripture says, "from glory to glory"!

Therefore, under a pagan government we are to return the "image" of it to it! However, we are to return the image of God to Him! For we are not our own image anymore but we are the very image of Christ under a pagan government (Democrat & Republican)! Our God has stamped His image upon us! We are now citizens of a new race of people, a new creation, Heaven bound and born again! Our liberty is in Christ, NOT in this world!

Saints, give Caesar's "image" back to him, but remember give God His image back to Him as we function in this pagan government. Fighting, hatred, lies, and malicious attitudes for the sake of "religious liberty" is not the image to return to our God, for how can we win souls for the kingdom with that image?

2 Corinthians 3:17–18 (KJV)

"Now the Lord is that Spirit: and where the Spirit of the Lord is, there is liberty. But we all, with open face

beholding as in a glass the glory of the Lord, are changed into the same image from glory to glory, even as by the Spirit of the Lord."

God Bless!

WAIT ON THE LORD, SAINTS!

In this day of demanding that we have everything *now*, we find ourselves many times scurrying around in circles. At the grocery store we find impulse items at the cashier's counter that entice us to buy those things that we really do not need. Department stores place high-volume items in the back of the store to compel us to walk through the store to get to them, setting the trap of having us once again buy those things we do not need and certainly had not planned to purchase.

Saints, many times we live our Spiritual lives in such a manner, whereby we lack patience and seek those things that we feel we need without any thought as to what God knows we need! Seeking our Father to provide what we want now without delay! After all, He is Jehovah-Jireh (our provider).

Mary and Martha's brother was ill and needed Jesus to come and heal him without delay, as they believed their brother Lazarus would die. When word got to Jesus about Lazarus's illness and pending death, Jesus looked to the disciples and stayed two more days where they were.

🪖 NUGGET ONE

Saints, Jesus often used situations as opportunities for teaching His disciples. He is teaching the Twelve with Him and all of us who are His disciples here today. The first lesson is patience and trust in Jesus. Jesus, in verse 4 of chapter 11 of John, was not surprised by the news. After all, Jesus is God! This was an opportunity to teach the disciples about the glory of God that Jesus the Son of God might be glorified!

Saints, whatever we ask of God we must know that He already knows, and He will answer when He is ready to answer! We must trust that His answer is best for us and timely for us as well.

Paul is another good example of this in that he asked God three times to heal his pain. God did not answer him until the third time he requested. Saints, sometimes God waits until we are ready to receive His answer. Waits until we can trust that His answer is for *His* best interest in our lives to serve Him. Not all things are expedient for us, and sometimes not even at the time we ask. That is why we must be prepared to accept things as they are:

Philippians 4:11–13 (KJV)

"Not that I speak in respect of want: for I have learned, in whatsoever state I am, therewith to be content. I know both how to be abased, and I know how to abound: every where and in all things I am instructed both to be full and to be hungry, both to abound and to suffer need. I can do all things through Christ which strengtheneth me."

Waiting for the Lord is to realize where our strength comes from! Both Mary and Martha had revealed their disappointment with Jesus in that He was late to come to Lazarus' rescue and Lazarus had died as a result.

NUGGET TWO

Saints, our Father is NEVER late, and the Son of God Jesus Christ is NEVER late either! Jesus knew that both sisters would be angry, but the teaching moment had begun for them as well. Jesus had to explain to Martha that He had power over death and life in that He said in verse 25:

> John 11:25–26 (KJV)
> *"Jesus said unto her, 'I am the resurrection, and the life: he that believeth in me, though he were dead, yet shall he live: And whosoever liveth and believeth in me shall never die. Believest thou this?'"*

Saints, all power is in the hand of Jesus! We must believe and trust in Him for our strength and our needs! We must trust Him even for our eternal life and power over death through Him! *"Believest thou this?"*

NUGGET THREE

Saints, as believers we must believe that Jesus knows what we need and when to act on our behalf. We must bear whatever trial with this reality in our hearts. Knowing that will give us reason to stand on God's Word and to grow in our trials with patience and confidence in an all-powerful God! We must not act like spoiled children of the Most High God by demanding our wants and desires but wait on Him and be prepared to receive the answer. David puts it this way:

Psalm 25:5 (KJV)
"Lead me in thy truth, and teach me: for thou art the God of my salvation; on thee do I wait all the day."

Lazarus had been dead for four days when Jesus asked where they had laid him. Then we see the shortest but one of the most powerful verses. That being **John 11:35,** *"Jesus wept"*!

🪙 LAST NUGGET

Saints, many will say to you that Jesus wept because His friend Lazarus had died, but that most certainly could not be true because in verse 4 Lazarus' death had not been from his sickness. Also, Psalms says that, "Precious in the sight of the Lord is the death of His Saints"! So why did Jesus weep? My friends, because those close to Him did not understand His teaching. They had missed the mark!

Today when we miss the mark by thinking that we can compel an all-knowing, merciful and loving God to do our bidding, we too make our Savior weep!

Jacob, who tried multiple times to get what he wanted at the time he wanted, came to repentance and finally realized that God is before all, above all and over all when he referred to God as the "God of hosts" and said this that I will leave for your understanding:

Hosea 12:6 (KJV)
"Therefore turn thou to thy God: keep mercy and judgment, and wait on thy God continually."

God Bless!

WHY DO YOU GO TO CHURCH, SAINTS?

Saints, what if someone were to ask you why you attend church. What would be your answer? What if the church greeter met you at the church entrance and asked you this very same question before you could come into the church?

What if your pastor met you at the front door of the church and asked you the same question? What would you tell your pastor?

J. Vernon McGee says that many people attend church to "tip their hats" to God. In other words, they may attend church under a false pretense of worship only to go back to a life of sin on Monday. Is that you Saints?

NUGGET ONE

Saints, Jeremiah was told by God to tell the Israelites that He sees them doing this very same thing! They were in the temple believing the temple would save them only to continue to live a life of sin on Monday!

Chapter 7 of Jeremiah is a warning given to them regarding their false worship and sinful living. A warning that God did not save them to continue in sin. Saints, this message was appropriate then as well as now!

God seeks genuine, non-ritualistic, sincere praise from His people even today. Ninety-nine-and-a-half percent is not sufficient praise for our great God who gave all, that we may have eternal life in His presence!

When we enter the church, we enter to praise, learn of and worship our Father in the name of Jesus Christ our Messiah! This form of praise and worship should be a life-changing experience such that we leave worship service different than when we arrived. More committed to our God by the revival of our hearts!

Many times, one can enter in with the expectation to leave at a certain time. Many churches have set start and ending times to attract members versus teaching members that they are to come to church not to "tip their hats to God" but open their hearts to Him no matter the time necessary to do so!

Revelation reminds us that we will be praising God all day and night! I wonder how many Saints then will be looking at their watches complaining . . .

NUGGET TWO

After the temple was rebuilt and the Ark of the Covenant found, thousands of Israelites came under the pretense of worship. Their plans, however, were to continue in sin. Ah but God had other plans! He told Jeremiah to meet them at the gate. Imagine thousands came to enter but God told Jeremiah to give them His message right there at the gate!

God saw their hearts and their sin and is not fooled by the "tipping of their hats"! What if Jesus met you at the front door of your church?

Jeremiah told them:

> **Jeremiah 7:9–11 (KJV)**
> *⁹ "Will ye steal, murder, and commit adultery, and swear falsely, and burn incense unto Baal, and walk after other gods whom ye know not; ¹⁰ And come and stand before me in this house, which is called by my name, and say, 'We are delivered to do all these abominations? ¹¹ Is this house, which is called by my name, become a den of robbers in your eyes? Behold, even I have seen it,' saith the LORD."*

Saints, are you just coming to church in ritualistic, time-sensitive worship to "tip your hat to God"? Are you seeking the choir to stimulate you to praise God instead of bringing your praise to church with you? Are you frustrated because the pastor gives a message that you think is too long and cuts into your time to get to other non-praising pursuits? Are you cheating your fellow brothers and sisters by not sharing your testimony of God's blessings in your life?

In your eyes, has your church become a "den of robbers"? If Jesus met you at the entrance of your church, what reason would you give Him as to why **_YOU_** are there? More importantly, what reason would Jesus see in **_YOUR_** heart? Would that confirm what you tell Him?

God Bless!

NUGGETS TO LIVE BY

4

PRAYER AND PATIENCE

NUGGETS TO LIVE BY

IT'S PRAYER TIME, SAINTS!

Saints, have you ever been invited to an invitation-only event? An event that required you to bring your invitation to receive access? A graduation ceremony or a party or a specific celebration?

Well, our Father has offered access to His throne by *invitation only*! You say, *What are you talking about, Pastor?* Well, Jesus' half-brother James puts it this way:

James 5:16 (KJV)
". . . The effectual fervent prayer of a righteous man availeth much."

🪨 NUGGET ONE

Saints, more than ever, in our current state of affairs we need earnest real prayers of faith! Faithful prayers that can move mountains! However, James points out that those prayers must come by invitation. In other words, one must consider the one that is praying.

James is reminding us that this prayer comes from a righteous man. Saints, a faithful prayer that availeth much has the blood of Christ all over it, for no man is righteous in and of himself. So, no man can stand at the throne of God in his own righteousness!

Saints, this man (in James) stands justified by the blood of Jesus at the throne! This man recognizes that he must become nothing that Christ becomes all! This man has faith to know that Christ's death, burial, and resurrection has made it possible for him as a blood-washed Christian to come with confidence to God's throne with all his cares and praises! That is why at the crucifixion the veil of the temple was torn from top to bottom, allowing blood-washed Christians total access to God's throne!

NUGGET TWO

Saints, it is the blood of Christ that justifies us by covering us with His righteousness! It is His blood that provides the invitation to the very throne of God! Simply put, we have all fallen short of the glory of God, Saints! But praise be to God He sent His son that by Him we are able to go to the throne where our Father waits to answer our prayers!

Saints, there is no other way but through Jesus! No one else can justify you before God! That is why when we pray, we pray presenting our invitation and saying that we are coming in "Jesus' name."

John 14:13-14 (KJV)
[13] *"And whatsoever ye shall ask in my name, that will I do, that the Father may be glorified in the Son. [14] If ye shall ask any thing in my name, I will do it."*

When we say in our prayers we are coming in Jesus' name, we are recognizing that we are powerless and have surrendered to the One who is powerful, and that is our Messiah, our Savior, our Shepherd, Jesus Christ! The above Scripture is our invitation to be present at the throne of God! That is why we say His powerful name! (John 14:13–14)

NUGGET THREE

Saints, the name of Jesus is POWERFUL! Look at the Scriptures below which reveal just how powerful His name is:

- The devils were powerless because of His name: **Luke 10:17**
- Demons were cast out in His name: **Mark 16:17–18**
- Healing was done in His name: **Acts 3:6, 3:16, 4:10**
- Salvation comes in His name: **Acts 4:12, Romans 10:13**

Ah, Saints, it's prayer time! Have you been washed in the blood? Then you have your own personal invitation to go *directly* to the throne! Saints, present your invitation and kneel *boldly and confidently in Jesus' name* before God in effectual, fervent prayer that it may availeth much for you!

Your invitation is in you and covers you; therefore, you do not have to go through anyone else or pray to anyone else. Just go directly to His throne where He waits for you . . .

Praise His Most Holy Name, Saints, *JESUS CHRIST*:

Colossians 3:17 (KJV)

17 "And whatsoever ye do in word or deed, do all in <u>the name of the Lord Jesus</u>, giving thanks to God and the Father <u>by him</u>."

God Bless!

NUGGETS TO LIVE BY

THE PRAYER OF ONE

Saints, do you know that the prayer of one can cause our Father to move on behalf of millions of His people? Scripture reminds us that *"the effectual fervent prayer of a righteous man availeth much"* **(James 5:16).**

Saints, there was one in some three million who prayed for deliverance of God's people from pending peril while the rest were afraid and lacked trust in God! Have you ever been there, Saints? Were you the one who prayed, or one of the millions who lacked trust in God to deliver the people because of strongholds preventing you from looking up rather than being captivated by the fear of the moment?

The Israelites found themselves in this predicament at the Red Sea. They were in terror believing they had been led away from Pharaoh only to die in the wilderness. That God was far from them, if He was present at all.

Saints, as children of God, do you ever feel abandoned by Him in the midst of a pending catastrophe? Have you felt your strength turn to weakness?

NUGGET ONE

While three million Israelites were complaining and crying out in fear, Moses was the only one to turn to God in prayer! He alone stepped up to the throne seeking the Lord's guidance. Imagine the enemy, ready to pounce and fellow believers giving up. Doesn't this happen even today?

To be sold out for the Lord is to step up in prayer when others have given up. Are you the first to complain or the first to refrain and trust in God through faithful prayer? Moses had assured the Israelites that God answered his prayer! That God would fight their battle and they only had to be still!

Saints, that is what God tells us even today . . . Amen?

NUGGET TWO

Saints, Scripture teaches us that our Creator does not faint or grow weary. By the prayer of one, God moved on behalf of three million! Scripture tells us that the angel of the Lord, and the cloud that led them, moved behind them, between them and Pharaoh's army, protecting and shielding them! Have you ever tried to get to a bear's cub? Trust me, there will be a fight on your hands which you will most assuredly loose!

God **_worked all night_** to make a way of escape for His people. Saints, rest easy; He will do the same for us today:

1 Corinthians 10:13 (KJV)
". . . God is faithful, who will not suffer you to be tempted above that ye are able; but will with the temptation also make a way to escape, that ye may be able to bear it."

Our God will also remove those strongholds that keep us from trusting and glorifying Him!

NUGGET THREE

The Israelites thought their problem was Pharaoh! However, their problem was their stronghold of lack of faith in trusting God. The Red Sea caused them to develop what I have referred to in the past as "stinkn' thinkn'"! Had the Red Sea not been there, they would have been fine . . . at least in their mind.

How many times, when all is fine for you, have you refrained from complaining? However, once your back is up against the wall, that wall causes you to develop "stinkn' thinkn'"? My friends, God can deliver you from this spiritual disease!

Look at what He did to their stronghold. He divided it by an east wind, defying the laws of nature! In doing so, leaving no doubt who did it! The Hebrew word for divide is *baqa*, as in splitting wood or rock. In other words, God split the water and the water from the ground for a mile to allow three million of His people to walk through on dry land!

Saints, God can release you of your stronghold and deliver you as well! All you have to do is trust and hope in Him alone! The world says that this defies nature, but, my friends, the sooner we realize that God is in control the better we will be!

Moses did not know how God would deliver them but all he had to do was trust and hope in God alone! Saints, we may find ourselves in such a quagmire that we are oblivious as to how God will deliver us. That's ok, because all we must know is that He will!

God had them walk on dry ground thus keeping their footing sure. Trusting in God and following the path He sets for you is to be blessed with sure footing as He makes your path smooth through your strongholds!

Saints, this all happened because of one sold out prayer warrior, Moses! Are you looking for a way of escape? My friend, Jesus is the answer. He prays for you and God makes a way of escape. Have you given your life to Him today?

Isaiah 40:28–31 (KJV)

"Hast thou not known? Hast thou not heard, that the everlasting God, the LORD, the Creator of the ends of the earth, fainteth not, neither is weary? There is no searching of his understanding. He giveth power to the faint; and to them that have no might he increaseth strength. Even the youths shall faint and be weary, and the young men shall utterly fall: But they that wait upon the LORD shall renew their strength; they shall mount up with wings as eagles; they shall run, and not be weary; and they shall walk, and not faint."

God Bless!

PRAYING WITHOUT FAITH IS REALLY BEGGING

Saints, while in eighth grade in Chicago, I had the responsibility of carrying the bus fare for my two brothers and one sister. In those days there was no school bus, only the Chicago Transit Authority.

However, there was "recess"! Saints, I really enjoyed recess and played from the beginning bell to the ending bell! Unfortunately, the money that I was responsible for to get my siblings and me home would always escape my pockets, socks, or jacket!

When school ended I would lead my brothers and sister to the corner bus stop, and there was this very nice lady who was the school's crossing guard. She knew me by name and seemed to always know when I had lost our bus fare. She would say, "George, are you OK?" I would respond, "I lost our bus fare again."

This nice crossing-guard lady would always have enough to give me for our bus fare! She never made me feel embarrassed or feel as if I had to beg. I really could count on her and knew that she was there for us.

One day over a family dinner with all my brothers and sister who came home from various colleges, we talked about this very nice crossing-guard lady. I shared with my parents about how she had always been there for us, especially on those days that the bus fare escaped from me. This was the first time I had confessed this to my parents. Some of you are probably laughing, but what eighth-grader would confess it, *ever*? Remember, spankings were sanctioned then!

My mom in all her wisdom said to all of us that she knew I had been losing our bus fare and that she had been giving this nice crossing-guard lady the money to hold for us on those days! *Now* it is OK to laugh!

NUGGET ONE

Saints, I now realize that they were looking out for us! That in those times of need we needed not to feel embarrassed or the need to beg. I had learned to confidently rely on this crossing guard. Saints, that is how we are to approach our God in times of need because He stands ready and able to supply all our needs:

> **Philippians 4:19 (AMP)**
> *"And my God will liberally supply (fill to the full) your every need according to His riches in glory in Christ Jesus."*

Saints, "every need—fill to the full"! Those who love His Son Jesus Christ and have given their lives to Him by His blood! That is why we can approach our Father in faith when we go to the throne of grace!

He knows what you stand in need of and is prepared to supply it if only you approach Him in faith, trusting and believing! Saints, this is not "name it and claim it"! "Name it and claim it" thinking is having faith in the object of your request. God wants us to have faith in Him, not the object of our request!

In Mathew chapter 9 there were two blind men that sought after Jesus for mercy. They were persistent in their seeking and followed Jesus into the house. It was there that Jesus turned and acknowledged them by asking them:

Matthew 9:28 (KJV)
"And when he was come into the house, the blind men came to him: and Jesus saith unto them, 'Believe ye that I am able to do this? They said unto him, Yea, Lord.'"

NUGGET TWO

Saints, Jesus challenged them as to their faith. Not "name it & claim it"! He asked them if they had faith in Him! Saints, we must follow the two blind men's example! They were persistent in seeking Christ, they knew Him as the Messiah, and most of all, they had faith in Him! No need to beg, Saints. Ask in Faith!

Saints, that is faith to trust that God will fill us to the full . . . wanting nothing!

Mark 11:22 (AMP)
"And Jesus, replying, said to them, 'Have faith in God [constantly].'"

God Bless!

NUGGETS TO LIVE BY

PRAYING WITHOUT PATIENCE IS FOR WIMPS

Saints, you ever find yourselves in situations where you make 9-1-1 calls to heaven? Those situations so dire that you find yourself seeking immediate help from God? Any delay from God would put you at a crossroads of your faith.

This crossroads threatens your hope and causes you to doubt. At the very least, any perceived delay from God to answer your prayer right away would turn your "concern" for your dire situation to the sin of "worry" over that situation.

NUGGET ONE

Saints, you are not alone in those moments! Remember the Israelites when they were delivered from Pharaoh and found themselves with their backs against the sea? They sent up 9-1-1 calls and lost patience to the point of doubting God and were prepared to surrender and go back into slavery.

How many times do you send up the same 9-1-1 call and ask for God to deliver you, and instead of being patient and waiting on the Lord, you begin by attempting to handle your situation alone apart from God? That, Saints, is a "wimpy" prayer!

Look at God's answer for the Israelites for such a "wimpy" prayer Saints:

Exodus 14:14–15 (AMP)
"The Lord will fight for you, and you shall hold your peace and remain at rest.
The Lord said to Moses, 'Why do you cry to Me? Tell the people of Israel to go forward!'"

NUGGET TWO

Saints, God told Moses to remind the Israelites that He would fight for them! That they were to hold their peace and remain at rest. After all, had God not proved to them that He would fight their battles? Has He not proven this to you as His child as well?

Moses was to remind them to be patient but not stand still. They were to stay focused and continue to go forward. Saints, when you face dire situations, they are not there to derail you. You are to continue to stand on the promises of our faithful Father and remain obedient in going forward on the battlefield!

No matter the answer or the time we receive the answer, God is always on time! After all, He created time and transcends time! One can only imagine that the Israelites looked forward and saw the sea and said to themselves, *Go forward?*

NUGGET THREE

Saints, in your own strength you cannot help but look at your situation as an insurmountable sea, but God promises to replace your weakness with His strength if only you will wait upon Him! Saints, there is no searching of His understanding! He alone knows your situation and the outcome of that situation just as He knew the sea that stood before the Israelites.

The Israelites were obedient to wait and go forward and God opened a path of deliverance for them and destruction for their enemies. Saints, He has made the same promise to you!

He says that if you just wait upon Him, He will cover you with His strength to make it, and you will peacefully soar as an eagle on the turbulence of those dire situations! *If only you would wait upon the Lord our Creator who never sleeps or is weary. Prayer without patience if for wimps, not you as a child of the King*:

Isaiah 40:28–31 (KJV)

"Hast thou not known? Hast thou not heard, that the everlasting God, the LORD, the Creator of the ends of the earth, fainteth not, neither is weary? There is no searching of his understanding. He giveth power to the faint; and to them that have no might he increaseth strength. Even the youths shall faint and be weary, and the young men shall utterly fall: But they that wait upon the LORD shall renew their strength; they shall mount up with wings as eagles; they shall run, and not be weary; and they shall walk, and not faint."

God Bless!

NUGGETS TO LIVE BY

THE PROMISE OF ANSWERED PRAYER

Saints, what an awesome God we have the privilege of serving! Our God stands prepared to answer our prayers and give us the desires of our heart!

> **Psalm 37:4 (KJV)**
> *⁴ "Delight thyself also in the LORD; and he shall give thee the desires of thine heart."*

Ah, Saints, but take note of the text. We must delight, and the Lord will "give"! We must "delight in the Lord"! A delight that will bring our desires to be consistent with the will of our Lord, not ours! How does one do this, Saints?

🪨 NUGGET ONE

We must delight in the very existence and perfection of our God. We must understand God's perfect will for our lives. Saints, as we walk with our Lord, we learn to embrace His will as we see that His will always proves to be better for us than anything that our flesh desires! When we embrace our Lord's will, we learn to delight in it and look forward to it in answered prayer! Just as Jesus did when He prayed and revealed His delight in His Father's will when He said to the Father, "not my will but thy will . . ."

NUGGET TWO

Saints, when we experience God's presence in our good and bad times and His grace and mercy for us as His children, we cannot help but delight in the relationship He has with us. We learn to rely on this relationship by prayer and obedience for as Lamentations reminds us, His grace and mercies are new every morning and sufficient for the day. How can one not delight in our Father?

Ah, but the question must be asked: are you reciprocating in the relationship by your obedience and reliance on God's will for you instead of yours? To delight is to do just that! After all, our Father delighted in us from the very beginning **(Prov. 8:28–31)**!

NUGGET THREE

Saints, how many of you have delighted in the Lord moving in your hearts to do His will? Recognizing that as you have walked with Him, you are many times astonished of how different your life has become? How you have changed in patience, controlling your tongue, your perspective of your enemies, your repulse of your fleshly life before you gave your life to Him, etc.? Recognizing how God has given you the desire to do His will:

Philippians 2:13 (KJV)
¹³ "For it is God which worketh in you both to will and to do of his good pleasure."

Saints, how can a Saint not delight in this?

NUGGET FOUR

Saints, we must not only delight in God's Word but delight in pursuing in its understanding and application in our lives. Psalm 1 reminds us that we are to "meditate in it day and night"! A Saint delighting in the Lord has an insatiable desire to study and meditate day and night and a desire to apply the Scriptures to his or her life for Jesus! Just going to church is not enough . . . **2 Timothy 2:15 and 2 Timothy 3:16!**

NUGGET FIVE

Finally, but not all-inclusive, Saints, a sold out Christian for our Lord delights in pleasing and serving Him! Saints, I would venture to say that if you have a problem in this area, it is probably rooted in one or all the previous four NUGGETS. Saints, if you are strong in delighting in all four NUGGETS, you cannot help but desire with delight to please and serve our God! I dare you!

Finally, those who delight in God will not ask for nothing but what will please God. Saints, our will is now lost in the very will of our Father, God!!

God Bless!

NUGGETS TO LIVE BY

THE PROMISE OF GRACE TO ENDURE

Saints, imagine with me training someone to take your position before you either move into a new position or retire. This replacement has never taken on such a challenge before and may be a little leery and perhaps somewhat intimidated because he has never done your position before. What would you tell him?

Paul had this very opportunity with his replacement when he gave this charge to his son in the ministry, Timothy! Look at what he told Timothy:

2 Timothy 2:1–3 (KJV)
¹ "Thou therefore, my son, be strong in the grace that is in Christ Jesus. ² And the things that thou hast heard of me among many witnesses, the same commit thou to faithful men, who shall be able to teach others also. ³ Thou therefore endure hardness, as a good soldier of Jesus Christ."

🪙 NUGGET ONE

Paul spoke from experience! You think Paul had to endure many obstacles on the road God enabled him to travel? Paul had never traveled this road before!

Saints, as we enter a new year, we too are traveling a road we have never traveled. As Christians, we are also guaranteed that we will face many obstacles on this new road . . . guaranteed, Saints!

Especially if you as you should, plan to do more for the Lord this year than you did last year! Obstacles will abound, Saints! Also, this message is not just for a pastor, it is a message for all ministers and those who are called to spread the Gospel! Hello, that is all of YOU, Saints! All Christians are responsible for the charge given by Jesus in Matthew 28:18-20 known as the Great Commission!

Let us look at our text, Saints. Paul gave excellent advice to Timothy that we need to take as we move into this new year of challenges. He told Timothy to *"be strong in the grace that is in Christ Jesus!"* Saints, the most important word in this statement is *in*!

🪙 NUGGET TWO

Paul knew that the grace that is in Jesus Christ is an enabling grace to endure and to overcome. A grace that causes believers to exercise our faith *"in"* Jesus Christ. Paul knew that Timothy had to learn more and more to rely on the grace *"in"* Christ to succeed! After all, Christ is the great overcomer!

As we face new challenges, Saints, we too must grow in this grace to endure and overcome to succeed this year. This grace is an active grace that should encourage us to do more for the Lord this year. It is not a grace of contentment but grace of endurance to succeed.

It is grace that when we realize how wretched we were before we accepted Jesus Christ, this grace of endurance convicted us to do the work of the Lord with a zeal, at the very least, matching the zeal when we were lost in sin! Look at what Paul said about this grace:

1 Corinthians 15:9–10 (KJV)
⁹ "For I am the least of the apostles, that am not meet to be called an apostle, because I persecuted the church of God. ¹⁰ But by the grace of God I am what I am: and his grace which was bestowed upon me was not in vain; but I laboured more abundantly than they all: yet not I, but the grace of God which was with me."

NUGGET THREE
Saints, Paul knew he had sinned horribly in persecuting Christians and the church. However, God had forgiven all his sins and called him to do His will! Saints, sound familiar? When we look in the mirror, can we say the same thing about our Lord's forgiveness? All of us have a story, a testimony of the mercy and forgiveness of our Lord, forgiving each of us for sin that we escaped damnation!

Paul said that the grace that was bestowed on him was not in vain. Was this same grace bestowed on YOU *in vain*? He also said that he labored more abundantly because of this grace! *Have you*? *Will you* in the next year? (*See Revelation 3:21!*)

God Bless!

NUGGETS TO LIVE BY

THE SECRET PRAYER OF A FATHER

Many times, fathers are seen as the breadwinners, scurrying off to their jobs, carrying the load of their families. His family members having no idea the load he carries. Perhaps thinking that he may be so busy he may not have time for them much less for God.

Psalm 119:62 tells us about a father by the name of David. David said

Psalm 119:62 (KJV)
"At midnight I will rise to give thanks unto thee because of thy righteous judgments."

My dad had two jobs for as long as I can remember. Leaving one and coming home to get a few hours rest and then off to his second job to help provide for us. Many times he was absent from church either working or getting rest to prepare for the next week of working.

However, I will never forget when my dad came to my first sermon. He was one of the loudest and most demonstrative people in the congregation, singing, praising, and exclaiming "Amens" during my sermon. It was then that I realized my dad knew God and had a relationship with Him! I found out that my dad had been studying with people in an in-home Bible study program. I wonder how many days when I thought he was resting between jobs my dad was praying to God for him and his family!

NUGGET ONE

Saints, David said *"At midnight I will rise to give thee thanks"*! There a father finds himself alone with God in sincere praise! Not standing amongst other men in the church but alone with God, sincerely offering praises for the grace and mercy God had showered upon him and his family.

When I ponder this as a father myself I can remember many a midnight I hit my knees thanking God for my family and His blessing that He showered upon us! All of them safe through college, unharmed, and living fruitful adult lives. However, it is something about being alone with God about one's family while the family is safely sleeping within the father's home.

David said, *"I will rise"*! Fathers, that means that he would physically demonstrate what his heart was doing and get out of bed and kneel down in a prayer of thanksgiving praise!

NUGGET TWO

Saints, I also know as a father there are times when we are alone with our God praying for God's presence and deliverance during those times our family may be going through such trials as finances, illnesses, or other trials that may drain our faith. That is when we as fathers sing to God as Paul and Silas did in the prison in **Acts 16**!

Fathers, do you know in those times God can give us a new song? Elihu told Job this when he tried to encourage him to call upon the Lord when others would not:

Job 35:9–10 (KJV)
"By reason of the multitude of oppressions they make the oppressed to cry: they cry out by reason of the arm of the mighty. But none saith, Where is God my maker, who giveth songs in the night..."

Saints, a father praying for his family alone with God will receive song in the midst of the trial! I cannot count the number of times I hit my knees heavily burdened with family trials only to begin humming and then bursting out in song. Songs such as *Amazing Grace*! Particularly, "Tis grace hath brought me safe thus far, and grace will lead me home..."

Those prayers are prayers of faith from a father in the midnight hour for his family. Trusting God's promise that those who pray in secret will be rewarded openly:

Matthew 6:5–6 (KJV)
"And when thou prayest, thou shalt not be as the hypocrites are: for they love to pray standing in the synagogues and in the corners of the streets, that they may be seen of men. Verily I say unto you, They have their reward. But thou, when thou prayest, enter into thy closet, and when thou hast shut thy door, pray to thy Father which is in secret; and thy Father which seeth in secret shall reward thee openly."

NUGGET THREE

Fathers, have you gotten out of your bed in the midnight hour to call upon the name of our God alone for you and your family? That is what Father's Day is all about! To first be alone with the best Father we will ever have . . . AMEN?

David was tired of being fearful of his enemies that he said this about his sleep:

Psalm 6:6 (AMP)
"I am weary with my groaning; all night I soak my pillow with tears, I drench my couch with my weeping."

Fathers, sometimes our worst enemy as a father is ourselves! I dare you to pray in the midnight hour alone with God and allow Him to reward you openly!

God Bless!

THE PERFECT WORK OF PATIENCE FOR THE APOSTLE PAUL

Saints, like Job who cried out to his adversaries to write down what he was about to say regarding the work of patience in his life in Romans 5:1–4, the apostle Paul wrote the work of patience in his life. However, there is a significant difference in Paul's writings.

Romans 5:1–4 (KJV)
[1] "Therefore being justified by faith, we have peace with God through our Lord Jesus Christ: [2] By whom also we have access by faith into this grace wherein we stand, and rejoice in hope of the glory of God.
[3] And not only so, but we glory in tribulations also: knowing that tribulation worketh patience; [4] And patience, experience; and experience, hope . . ."

The Roman's text is speaking from the perspective of this side of the cross versus the Old Testament writings of Job, Abraham, and Noah.

Paul makes it clear that the work of patience will have a substantial work in those who are truly justified by the blood of

Jesus Christ! The blood that was shed on the cross for the work of our salvation!

Paul is speaking to those who have truly given themselves to Christ by trusting Him one hundred percent! Those who truly understand that their sins have been forgiven and that Christ now sits at the right hand of the Father interceding on our behalf. In other words, one who professes his belief and doubts or does not totally believe would not be able to have the perfect work of patience in his or her life.

> **James 1:3–4 (KJV)**
> *³ "Knowing this, that the trying of your faith worketh patience.*
> *⁴ But let patience have her perfect work, that ye may be perfect and entire, wanting nothing."*

NUGGET ONE

Saints, the apostle Paul in Romans is pointing out that a truly blood-washed Christian would have a totally different perspective of his trials and sufferings. A truly justified Christian who allows patience to have her perfect work in him would view any trials and sufferings as neither hopeless nor have any ability to hurt him.

Instead, trials and sufferings for a truly blood-washed Christian is a source of purpose and meaning in our life as we walk with God! A truly blood-washed Christian would trust God enough to know that his trial is allowed by God for a purpose to draw him closer to God by the experience and to mature his Christian character by that same experience.

NUGGET TWO

Saints, some of you may be saying to yourself that is difficult to realize in some of our trials. Well, that is exactly the point the apostle is addressing! Paul is reminding us that a truly justified Christian knows that no matter the trial, as His child we are always under our Father's care and under His watchful eye.

That our Father allows both good and bad in our lives for a reason. A truly justified Christian may not be able to see the reason as he is amid his trial or suffering, but he is confident that God's presence and purpose will be revealed in due time and it will be the right time! That is why in a truly justified person's prayer, he is confident enough to thank God for his trial and thank God in advance for God's pending deliverance. As Job said in this life or the next!

That is why Paul says that we "glory in tribulation," saints!

Saints, in Acts 16:16–40 we see the experience that Paul may be referring to in Romans. Many of you may know this text. Paul and Silas had been lied about to the magistrates by those who were making money off the works of a demon-possessed damsel.

A multitude revolted against them and they were found guilty and beaten and placed in the depth of the prison. Never once do we see that either Paul or Silas complained. Not once do we see that either was worried; instead, they "gloried in their tribulation"!

NUGGET THREE

Saints, they began to pray and sing songs! Saints, I believe they had every confidence that God was watching over them and that God allowed them to be stripped of their cloths, beaten and thrown into prison for a reason! Saints, can you just hear their prayer thanking God in advance for His pending delivery? Can't you hear it?

Singing songs of praise to an awesome, great God! Can't you hear it?

Saints, have you prayed to God amid your trial, confident that He will deliver you? Thanking Him for allowing this trial to draw you closer to Him? Praising Him alone in song even while tears of joy roll down your cheeks? Have you Saints?

Paul and Silas did not know how they would be delivered, but they had every confidence God would be on time!

Saints, not only did God save them, but the text says that He also saved all those who were listening to them pray and praise God! Eventually God used Paul and Silas to win the guard and his family to Christ!

Ah, Saints, have you allowed patience to have her perfect work in you to the point that you too "glory in your tribulation"? Or do you grieve, strike back, and lament and scare those unbelievers watching you from Christ by your demeanor?

Are you truly justified in the blood Saints?

God Bless!

THE PERFECT WORK OF PATIENCE FOR GOD'S FIRST EVANGELIST

Saints, God's first evangelist had a tough duty! That evangelist was Noah. Noah is mentioned in Genesis 6 and we find that in 2 Peter 2:5, Noah is referred to as a "preacher of righteousness"!

Saints, many may believe that Noah stood alone in his ministry as for one hundred twenty years of preaching he only converted seven people. All seven were his family! But Saints, Noah had allowed God's patience to have its perfect work in him to complete his mission!

Saints, Noah was ready for his assignment. Genesis alerts us to a few things that confirm his readiness.

NUGGET ONE

Genesis 6:9 says that Noah "walked with God." My friends, that means that Noah had a personal, intimate relationship with God! That he relied and depended on God for everything. That he trusted God in good and bad times, for he knew God and God knew him! He knew God so well that while others thought he was alone in his preaching, Noah knew he was never alone.

Saints, can you say that in your walk with God He can count on you and you can count on Him in your calling to exercise your God given gift? Whether it be ushering, preaching, greeting, choir, etc.? Are you devoting your time in walking with God or are you only giving God your ten- to fifteen-minute "break time"? Noah, through his walk with God, allowed patience and endurance to have its perfect work in him!

NUGGET TWO

The text further says that Noah was "a just man and perfect." Saints, that does not mean that Noah was without sin! Noah needed God as much as we all do! However, in this text, God's Word is letting us know that Noah was complete in his maturation process with God. Noah was not a child in his spiritual growth and he was ready for God to use him.

Ah, Saints, are you there yet? Are you maturing enough in your walk with God that God can use you? Are you maturing enough in your walk with God that God can count on and trust you with a mission? Saints, we all as redeemed sinners have an evangelist ministry and commandment:

Matthew 28:18–20 (KJV)

[18] *"And Jesus came and spake unto them, saying, 'All power is given unto me in heaven and in earth.* [19] *Go ye therefore, and teach all nations, baptizing them in the name of the Father, and of the Son, and of the Holy Ghost:* [20] *Teaching them to observe all things whatsoever I have commanded you: and, lo, I am with you always, even unto the end of the world. Amen.'"*

NUGGET THREE

Saints, again have you spent more time in your walk with God lately or only giving Him ten to fifteen minutes a day of break time? Scripture says that in Noah's day the world was corrupt and filled with violence! *Sound familiar?*

Saints, this is *exactly* the time to spend more time with our Lord! Noah was steadfast in his mission and time with God. Noah preached, built an ark, and gathered animals that he would be responsible for during his mission. Noah was doing more than one thing at a time for God. Are you? Can you do multiple things simultaneously for God? Or are you sitting in the church pew doing nothing to further the gospel? In your church, is there twenty percent of the congregation doing eighty percent of the work? Which part are you? Nowhere does it say Noah complained about doing double duty for more than one hundred twenty years! Do you?

Finally, Noah stayed strong amid stormy seas. Imagine Noah experiencing forty days of storms! Wow, rough seas, scared animals, dark nights, and trees, buildings and unbelievers floating in the water! Yet he stayed the course! Knowing that his trust was in God's Word and promise!

Saints, when you are amid your stormy sea, who do you trust? Have you let patience have its perfect work in you that you intimately trust in God? Trusting in His grace and mercy because you have walked with Him enough to know Him as He knows you? Or are you just being introduced to God through your trial?

My friends, NOW is the time to know Him! For just as this has happened in Noah's day it will happen in our day. They waited until the flood came and it was TOO LATE! The door of the ark was closed! My friends don't let the door of heaven close on *you*!

Matthew 24:37–39 (KJV)
^{37} "But as the days of Noah were, so shall also the coming of the Son of man be.
^{38} For as in the days that were before the flood they were eating and drinking, marrying and giving in marriage, until the day that Noah entered into the ark, ^{39} And knew not until the flood came, and took them all away; so shall also the coming of the Son of man be."

Saints, have you allowed patience to have its perfect work in you?

God Bless!

THE PERFECT WORK OF PATIENCE FOR JOB (PART 1)

Saints, James, the oldest half-brother of Jesus wrote in his epistle to the twelve tribes scattered abroad words of encouragement. In Chapter 5 verses 10 and 11, James mentions for encouragement "the patience of Job."

During the time of this writing, the people were facing many tremendous trials. Some of them we are facing yet today. The first Christian martyr had taken place as Deacon Stephen had been stoned to death. Jewish Christians were fleeing Jerusalem as Saul was persecuting them by dragging them out of the synagogues and into courts to be imprisoned and put to death. James (not Jesus' half-brother) the apostle was killed, and Peter had barely escaped death.

Saints, during all this James sought to encourage them by letting them know that under tremendous trials they needed tremendous patience. Also, that patience needed to have its perfect work in them.

NUGGET ONE

Saints, today as we witness tremendous trials involving our churches and our fellow brothers and sisters, we need to take pause and look at the "patience of Job" as well. We are witnessing people being gun downed in church buildings. God's laws being ignored by our government. The poor and the elderly being dismissed by the greed of our government. Unarmed minorities being gunned down in the streets by those hired to protect and serve without any judicial remedy offered to their families . . .

Saints, James knew that true Christians need to have the patience of endurance! We too must have the same patience during these times and the more tremendous the trial, the more tremendous the work of patience in the true Christian is needed!

How, you ask? Let us look at Job.

Job was about forty to fifty years old when in one day he lost all his children and his wealth in one day! Job also lost his health as he had sores all over his body so bad that his friends could not recognize him. To add insult to injury, Job's wife told Job to give up and "curse God and die"!

As if that was not enough, Job's "friends" told Job that the reason all these trials were piling up on Job was because he was in sin, arrogant, and empty! With these "friends" who needs enemies?

NUGGET TWO

Ah, Saints, the first Nugget to understanding how to allow patience to have its perfect work in us is how Job handled Eliphaz and his wife!

Job 2:10 (KJV)

¹⁰ "But he said unto her, 'Thou speakest as one of the foolish women speaketh. What? Shall we receive good at the hand of God, and shall we not receive evil? In all this did not Job sin with his lips.'"

Saints, only one who has a relationship with God would understand that we all will have trials and the tougher the trial, the more to gain in allowing patience to have its perfect work within us!

But Job's response to his friends is where we need to take notice. Job focused on God, NOT his friends' false accusations! Job responded to their accusation that God could not be found during his current tremendous trials.

NUGGET THREE

Saints, the first step that Job is teaching us is that HE KNEW GOD KNEW HIM! That in the good and the bad, God had a sincere relationship with him. Saints, as you go through your trials, can you honestly say that God knows you? Have you devoted your life to him that by your life God knows you as His child?

Job said, God knows the way he takes that God has concern for and appreciates it! That God pays attention to what he is going through and with God he will come through this trial refined as pure gold!

Why? Because God knew that Job's footsteps followed the steps of God! That Job had never turned aside! Job had not gone back on God's commandments and Job esteemed and treasured the very Word of God more than food!

Saints, can you say that God knows you this way? Tremendous trials require a tremendous effort that God may know you as His child! Many times, we witness those who are not prepared for tremendous trials because they have not committed to God and His Word. Saints, how can one expect today to have the Holy Spirit to teach and remind you of our Father's Word when you are not praying, studying, attending a Bible teaching church, and growing in the knowledge of God?

Job did, and he had every confidence that God knew him as His child. ***Does God know you that way?***

Job 23:10–12 (AMP)

[10] "But He knows the way that I take [He has concern for it, appreciates, and pays attention to it]. When He has tried me, I shall come forth as refined gold [pure and luminous]. [11] My foot has held fast to His steps; His ways have I kept and not turned aside. [12] I have not gone back from the commandment of His lips; I have esteemed and treasured the Words of His mouth more than my necessary food."

God Bless!

THE PERFECT WORK OF PATIENCE FOR JOB (PART 2)

Saints, many of our favorite spirituals are written such as *The battle Is the not Ours, it's the Lord's, Amazing Grace,* and *I Will Trust the Lord* as responses to tremendous trials and sufferings of God's people.

These songs remind us that in the darkest of times, our God makes His presence the clearest, as a bright diamond that a jeweler sits on a dark cloth. The message in this situation is that we learn to realize God alone is our source of strength!

The second point in the perfect work of patience for Job is that "one's patience is tied to one's faith of things not seen" (2 Cor. 4:15–18).

NUGGET ONE

Saints, Job was in the midst of a wife, "friends," and poor health that attempted to have him focus on things temporal, but Job flipped the script on them! Saints, how often does the world and the worldly try to get you to change your focus to worldly circumstances away from eternal promises?

Asaph found himself in the same situation being discouraged about the wealthy and powerful having no problems while with God's follower's trials continued to mount. But Asaph said, ". . . until I went into the sanctuary of God then understood I their end" (Ps. 73:17). My friends, God had changed Asaph's focus away from the present to the eternal promise!

In Job 19:23–27 we see Job finally crying out to his accusers who were trying to get him to focus on the temporal an important message. That message is relevant for us even today!

NUGGET TWO

Job says what he was about to say should be put in a book, chiseled on a rock forever! Oh, Saints, Job was about to teach them something and he is teaching many even to this day!

Saints, Job cried out to those who told him to curse God and die and that God was not to be found, "I know my Redeemer liveth"! Job was focusing on eternal promises not current circumstances! Job had total confidence and faith in The Redeemer! Saints, where is your focus in trials or even in good times?

Keep in mind, Saints, at this point God had not given any words of comfort, encouragement, guidance, or a promise of a better future for Job, but Job held tightly to the profession of his faith! Do you? (Heb. 10:23) On this side of the cross we have such words of comfort, encouragement, guidance, and the promise of a better future in writing! Our Father's Bible! Therefore, we are without excuse for not holding on!

NUGGET THREE

Job said that God would redeem him in this life or the next! He made sure to let them know that he trusted God and he knew his future. Saints, because despite what the worldly say, God is a faithful God to His people without question!

Job was so certain and confident that he further said when he finally sees God, Job would not be a stranger to Him. Wow, Saints, when you get to Heaven will you have to be introduced to God? Will that be the first time you are trying to get a sincere relationship with Him? Job will not be a stranger to God because he had a sincere relationship with God while on Earth. Do you?

Finally, Saints, Job said, "My reins be consumed within me." My friends, I can only imagine that Job was looking up to Heaven in front of his worldly accusers when he said this. My friends, he was saying that he had a burning desire within him to see God! Ah, Saints, do you have a burning desire within you to see God?

Saints, Job was focusing on the unseen! He had total faith in the unseen in the midst of his tremendous trial! What does that teach us as we go through promised trials as children of the God?

2 Corinthians 4:17–18 (KJV)
17 "For our light affliction, which is but for a moment, worketh for us a far more exceeding and eternal weight of glory; 18 While we look not at the things which are seen, but at the things which are not seen: for the things which are seen are temporal; but the things which are not seen are eternal."

God Bless!

NUGGETS TO LIVE BY

THE PERFECT WORK OF PATIENCE FOR THE SAINTS

Saints, I witnessed a sermon where the preacher asked the congregation what they would do if a bank president opened his vault and freely offered them as much money as they wanted? Many of them gave such answers as "I would fill my trunk," "fill my big purse," "go get a truck and fill it," and on and on.

Then the preacher asked, "What if I told you that one person went into the vault and just took a nickel?" Many were astounded, laughing saying "only a nickel?"

Saints, our Heavenly Father has a vault too loaded with everything we need to walk this Christian journey. Help such as the peace and joy of Christ! Including patience and the work thereof. Yet Saints, many of you struggle needlessly from the lack of patience because you chose to function on a nickel's worth instead of seeking all that our Heavenly Father offers to us His children!

Saints, God's Word assures us that those Saints who keep the Word of His patience will be kept from the Tribulation!

Revelation 3:10 (KJV)
¹⁰ "Because thou hast kept the Word of my patience, I also will keep thee from the hour of temptation, which shall come upon all the world, to try them that dwell upon the earth."

NUGGET ONE

Saints, James speaks of the "the perfect work of patience" in chapter one:

James 1:3–4 (KJV)
³ "Knowing this, that the trying of your faith worketh patience.
⁴ But let patience have her perfect work, that ye may be perfect and entire, wanting nothing."

Allowing the perfect work of patience to grow us into "perfect and entire" Saints "wanting nothing" is crucial to seeking our crowns! The very crowns that we will be casting at our Master's feet!

NUGGET TWO

Saints, we all have issues with patience. Some more so than others but we are all without excuse as our God freely offers as much as we desire and certainly would need. The question is, are you only operating on a nickel's worth of God-given patience?

Saints, do you need to return to the Master's vault? The perfect work of patience should develop such Christian qualities such as ENDURANCE and STEADFASTNESS! The fruit of these Christian qualities will lead the Saints into a sincere worship of our God!

James 1:3–4 (AMP)
³ "Be assured and understand that the trial and proving of your faith bring out endurance and steadfastness and patience.
⁴ But let endurance and steadfastness and patience have full play and do a thorough work, so that you may be [people] perfectly and fully developed [with no defects], lacking in nothing."

God Bless!

www.ingramcontent.com/pod-product-compliance
Lightning Source LLC
Chambersburg PA
CBHW030106100526
44591CB00009B/289